PHOTOGRAPHY
CRISIS OF HISTORY

PHOTOGRAPHY
CRISIS OF HISTORY

Joan Fontcuberta, ed.

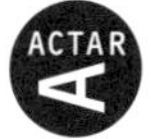

6 REVISITING THE HISTORIES OF PHOTOGRAPHY
Joan Fontcuberta

18 Ian Jeffrey

30 Marie-Loup Sougez

42 FROM THE "NEWHALL SCHOOL" TO THE
"HISTORIES" OF PHOTOGRAPHY:
EXPERIENCES AND PROPOSALS FOR
THE FUTURE Bernardo Riego

58 GOOD-BYE, MR. NEWHALL José Antonio Navarrete

74 REFLECTIONS FOR A NEW HISTORY OF
PHOTOGRAPHY Carmelo Vega

84 THE HISTORY OF PHOTOGRAPHY, A HISTORY OF
PHOTOGRAPHIES Daniel Girardin

94 REFLECTIONS ON THE HISTORY OF
PHOTOGRAPHY Boris Kossoy

108 WRITING HISTORY "OPENING THE CRACKS"
Mounira Khémir

120 UNCOMFORTABLE REFLECTIONS Teresa Siza

134 Joan Naranjo

144 THE FIELD OF DEPTH
Henning Steen Wettendorff

156 THE MECHANICAL ART: SOME HISTORIC
DEBATES ON ART AND PHOTOGRAPHY
Andrea Kunard

176 RECYCLING OF REALITY: SEARCHING FOR
A HISTORICAL INFRASTRUCTURE FROM
PARADOX TO PAROXYSM Johann Swinnen

190 THE INSTANT OF HISTORY Vincent Lavoie

208 REFLECTIONS FOR A NEW HISTORY OF
PHOTOGRAPHY Carmelo Vega

218 THE PHOTOGRAPHY OF HISTORY – THE
HISTORY OF PHOTOGRAPHY. SOME
PERIPHERAL OBSERVATIONS
Hubertus von Amelunxen

224 PHOTOGRAPHY, LABORATORY OF A HISTORY
OF MODERNITY
André Gunthert

236 HISTORY OF PHOTOGRAPHY
Selected bibliography
Mariona Fernández

REVISITING THE HISTORIES OF PHOTOGRAPHY

Joan Fontcuberta

Both in the region of North America and in the most advanced countries of Europe, the seventies signified for photography the beginning of its double institutionalization as a matter of academic and museological interest. It can be argued that even before then photography was already being treated as a subject of scholarly study and being collected in museums. This is true; but it was from the seventies on that it became widely implanted among the canonizing structures of knowledge and culture. Such a process of diffusion and valorization was of course accompanied by the incorporation of photography into the realm of contemporary art and the emergence of a dynamic market for photography as an art object.

The need to rethink its history that photography has periodically felt also dates from that time. In a process of cyclical return, the experts have questioned our understanding and interpretation of the past, and these critical phases have corresponded with certain specific problems which, although perfectly legitimate, have been inscribed only as subliminal messages on the margins of the official discourse, as if the historiographic debate served in fact to instrumentalize a series of undeclared interests. If we look back now at the proceedings of symposiums and monograph publications it is not hard to see the presence of those conjunctural theoretical emergencies. For example, if we leaf through the special issue entitled "Quelle histoire la Photographie!" prepared by the *Cahiers de la Photographie* team in 1981 [1], we can perceive the tension between a historiography that utilizes photography to explain life and another that concentrates on

1 *Les cahiers da la Photographie*, no. 3, 3rd quarter 1981, Paris.

explaining photography itself. This second option ends up imposing itself: in the text which probably contains the highest density of doctrine, Jean-Claude Lemagny declares that History has "cannibalized" photography, exhorts us to stop confusing a history-by -means-of-photography with the genuine History of Photography, and concludes with a call to give our attention to "a photography that will no longer be an auxiliary science but a mode of being of History". Lemagny, indisputably one of the intellectual beacons of European photography in recent times, championed the differential condition of a "creative photography" and, in line with this, the importance of ensuring that this type of art received the specific treatment it required, something he himself was so ably and actively promoting from his position as curator of photography in the prints section of the Bibliothèque Nationale de France.

Another example: in 1979 the Art Institute of Chicago organized a series of lectures under the eloquent title "Towards the New Histories of Photography", of which one of the most extensively reproduced and quoted was the paper presented by Professor Carl Chiarenza, "Towards an Integrated History of Picturemaking" [2]. There Chiarenza defended the unity of visual culture in spite of the different procedures for the production of images, and rejected the ghetto of a separate history for photography, calling instead for a general

2 Reproduced in *Afterimage,* February 1979, Rochester, and in *Reading into Photography,* Thomas F. Barrow, Shelley Armitage and William E. Tydeman (eds), University of New Mexico Press, Albuquerque, 1982.

history of art that would accept in full and on terms of equality the other traditional disciplines. With the perspective allowed us by time we can see those postulates in a logic that no one would dispute, but an attentive reading of the circumstances reveals the debate between art and photography that preceded the irruption of Postmodernism. Newhall wrote a history that suited the collectors and the curators of museums of modern art, and Chiarenza began to prepare the ground for the collections of contemporary art.

These successive visits to history bear witness to the different cultural and ideological frames through which photography itself has passed. I would now like to propose, therefore, a new debate on the history of photography but one which will differ from other previous debates in setting out from the assumption of a very precise and explicit frame, a frame which at the same time defines a crucial point in the evolution of photography.

The fact is that photography has arrived at the year 2000 beset by an apparent crisis of identity. The vertiginous technological changes all around us, together with the political and economic context that underpins these, has transformed the genesis and the nature of the photographic image to such an extent as to legitimate every uncertainty as to its current status. There still remains the gesture of the photographer, and there still remains too the appearance of the final image as iconic product, but the route between the one and the other now passes through an unrecognizable landscape. Certain influential figures –such as Cartier-Bresson– have insisted in claiming that "photography has not changed since its origins, other than in the technique, which is what least interests us". This amounts to saying: keep calm, there is nothing going on. But the fact is that something is going on. What is important is not whether good old Henri could still find spare parts for his Leica, or if anyone would still develop his rolls of black and white film. The important questions are of a different kind. I offer here only a few of these, by way of illustration: with the concentration of giant media groups, would Henri be tolerated in his necessary independence? Given the dominance of the "people" press, does the *grand auteur* report still make sense? Will his photographs still be credible in the future? Would Henri give up his sense of his testimonial and narrative role for a purely ornamental one? Would his images be able to move a public brought up on video games and the Internet? Would he be scandalized at the digital "correction" of the mistakes in his shots? Can the "decisive instant" have any meaning for an audience habituated to the synthetic image and to virtual reality?

Photography has modified the protocol with industry, with science, with advertising, with journalism, with communication, with art, with everyday life... The whole ethical and aesthetic basis has been subverted. The landscape is decidedly unrecognizable, so unrecognizable that some, the most radical, are now speaking of the death of photography, while others, more moderate, introduce a new and necessarily ambiguous category: that of post-photography (a curious denomination that lies very close to another term: that of post-history). And a little reflection shows us that while those new technologies constitute the most visible causes of change, they are very far from being the only or even the most decisive causes. The dramatic metamorphosis from the grain of silver to the pixel represents nothing more than a screen which conceals the evolution taking place in the whole framework that provided photography with a cultural, instrumental and historical context.

The reasons for the instability of our conceptions of the photographic are numerous, and it is not my purpose to explore them in these lines, but I cannot avoid offering a brief note in passing. In photography, two facets have necessarily co-existed, perfectly fused and inseparable: on the one hand, the image as visual information; on the other, the physical support or medium, its objectual dimension. The daguerreotype as the starting point for the images produced by the camera was not an image fixed on a plate but a plate that embodied an image; its material presence was thus inevitable. The subsequent tendency, prompted by practical considerations, was towards the development of ever lighter supports. However, all through the course of history certain social uses or certain focuses have privileged one component or the other; in the realm of the archive, for example, the information aspect prevails, while in that of the museum, in contrast, it is the objectual aspect. What digital technology does is to accentuate the divide between image and support, between information and object. To say it in other words, digital technology has effectively dematerialized photography, situating it in a new configuration that will prohibit its access to certain past territories and promote the exploration of others. Photography has now become information in the pure state, content without matter whose power to fascinate will come to be governed by other factors. Issues of meaning will take precedence over issues of representation. It is hardly surprising, then, that in the realm of artistic expression digital photography should be unfavourable to certain developments of a formalist nature while accentuating others of a narrative and conceptual nature.

In any case, that crisis of identity is bound up with the different ways of narrating events, which places us in the binomial of the interdependent relationship between identity and history. The different ways of explaining the past call for a sifting of data and thus the presumption of certain criteria of "mîse en histoire" that in turn imply the creation of certain canons. The formulations of what we understand by photography define our object of study, at the same time as the historical interpretation legitimates a certain "way of being" of the photographic. This being so, the crisis of identity cannot then be seen as in any way separate from a crisis of the historiographic models on which our understanding of photography has been grounded. It follows, then, that what we are immersed in now is not so much a crisis of identity as a crisis of history.

A crisis of history of which we are, moreover, fully aware, and one that we regard not only from the academic but also from the creative perspective. History provides a frame of reference that simultaneously grounds our relationships with the heritage on the one hand and with contemporary creation on the other. The relation between history and the heritage is perfectly clear and there is no need to go into it at length: at the same time, the incidence of history on creative work tends to be overlooked, and this gives rise to a grave error, because there can be no real creation without a historical consciousness.

In the eighties we witnessed an especially intense phenomenon of the exploitation of the history. Under the scrutiny of the retroactive gaze of the artist, the past became not so much a source of inspiration as a source of material to be worked with. Recognizable images drawn from an iconic tour of the history of photography or even whole styles were subject to quotation, appropriation, reproduction, plagiarism, remake or pastiche, according to the degree of radicalism of artists who have preferred to work with the repertoire of images which preceded them, postponing contact with a universe of things and of facts. We all remember the duplicates of Walker Evans produced by Sherrie Levine, or the false collections of "masterpieces" presented by Joachim Schmid and Adib Fricke, or of Wolfgang Vollmer and Ulrich Tillmann. Over and above their ironic stance, these projects are in their entirety doubly relevant here because they possess the value of showing us that just as every image derives from some other image that preceded it, so all histories, too, derive from other histories.

These cases have, in short, amounted to a series of intellectually ingenious games with history, games which are symptomatic of that generic urge to revisit critically our interpretation of the past. But even if this urge is not so rigorously explicit, every creative work is based, in the very origin of its development, on a historical model, and in due course requires validation within that model. In the light of this, I want to insist that an understanding of history and the questions that arise from this are not only a subject of study for the specialists but also a personal baggage of data that are both necessary and useful in the elaboration of the images themselves. This underpins not only the need for a historical consciousness on the part of the creator but also, and above all, the practical significance that history assumes for the creator (creator here is to be understood as not only the person who specifically takes on the role of artist but everyone who contributes, in the form of images, to a certain visual culture). Within these parameters, a selection of specialists have been invited to offer their reflections on the state of the historiographic question in photography. Given that the debate could have been opened up in a number of possible directions, a common programme of eight points was drawn up with the aim of providing guidelines for the various critical itineraries; having said this, the contributors were by no means obliged to adhere to these, but were encouraged to respond with complete freedom. These eight points are as follows:

1) To begin with, there might be some value in establishing a before and an after Beaumont Newhall, the photo-historian who has exercised the greatest influence. The history of photography before Newhall is no more than a chronology of facts articulating a bare account of the evolution of certain techniques and the social effects of these; after Newhall, photography becomes an autonomous object for history, which now seeks to engage with its aesthetic specificity. But even so, the impression remains of an overwhelming mass of data without any underlying theoretical structure with which to interpret these and endow them with meaning.

We have to ask ourselves, then, if there has as yet been a real history of photography, or only its archaeology?

2) Newhall's model is the one that has in effect enjoyed the most extensive implantation, as witnessed by the fact that the majority of museum collections are based on his criteria. Newhall established the principal canon for the history of photography, the maximum

principle of authority. John Szarkowski, curator of photography at the MoMA for many years, corroborated this when he observed that the mere inclusion in Newhall's study of certain photographs or photographers automatically made these "classics". To criticize Newhall is thus at the same time to pay homage to him. His text basically presents the history of a technique that made possible a series of different modes of representation. What are the problems that emerge from this approach?

3) Let us take a wider look at the ranks of the classic historians (Eder, Newhall, Taft, Lécuyer, Gersheim, Scharf...) and at those of the generation that followed them (Gilardi, Rosenblum, Hassner, Lemagny, Frizot...). Histories, like any other human product, are governed by conventions, beliefs and circumstances of time and of place. The deconstruction of the historiographic discourse thus becomes an indispensable previous condition. What are the principal filters –cultural, ideological and political– that have determined the dominant historiographic models?

4) The History of photography is fragmented in the multiplicity of possible histories. Reducing the scope of analysis gives greater coherence in the premisses at the cost of renouncing a more transverse perspective. Can photography still be studied as an autonomous discipline, or is it more productive to look at it in its applications in other fields (journalism, advertising, art, anthropology, leisure, etc.)?

5) Normally we tend to think of the history of photography as a history of photographers and as a result subordinate the articulation of the historical method to the notion of attribution (this is a criterion borrowed from the history of art). Even if we consider it plausible,

this option disregards the enormous contingents of anonymous images or the very possibility of utilizing alternative historical units (for example, the photographic project). Which, then, is to prevail: a history of photographers or a history of images? Are these two approaches mutually exclusive or complementary?

6) There seems to be an irreconcilable divorce between a historiographic approach which privileges the information that photography gives us about reality and another which privileges the information that reality gives us about photography. Should photography be an instrument of study or an object of study? Is a social history of photography compatible with an aesthetic history, a history of uses with a history of forms?

7) Various European countries, to say nothing of whole continents, have been left on the fringes of the histories of photography. In many histories of photography, the omissions are actually more important than the inclusions.

The fact that a superb portraitist such as Seydou Keita works in Bamako gives him a far smaller chance of figuring in the history of photography than some mediocrity living in Paris, New York or one of the other great cities, which act as very effective platforms of projection. And in addition to this geographical discrimination there are many others on grounds of sex or of social position. How are we to produce a "politically correct" history of photography? How are we to open it up to the minorities, to disadvantaged groups, to the so-called Third World...?

8) Does history make photography or is it photography that produces history? Walter Benjamin wrote of the need to rethink photogra-

phy and history together, because what made an event historicizable was its technical reproducibility (its fixing in a photograph). The language of photography articulates history, in the measure that history bestows meaning on photography. In line with these premisses, how are we to address the history of photography?

The texts that follow represent different ways of revisiting history, and put forward ideas that will undoubtedly prove very useful in bringing new light to historical studies with a bearing on photography. They will help to place us in a position from which to overcome with greater surety that crisis of history in which we find ourselves. A crisis that, far from fearing, we should welcome as a factor of stimulus, of thought and of creativity.

Joan Fontcuberta is a photographer, university lecturer and chief editor of the magazine *Photovision*.

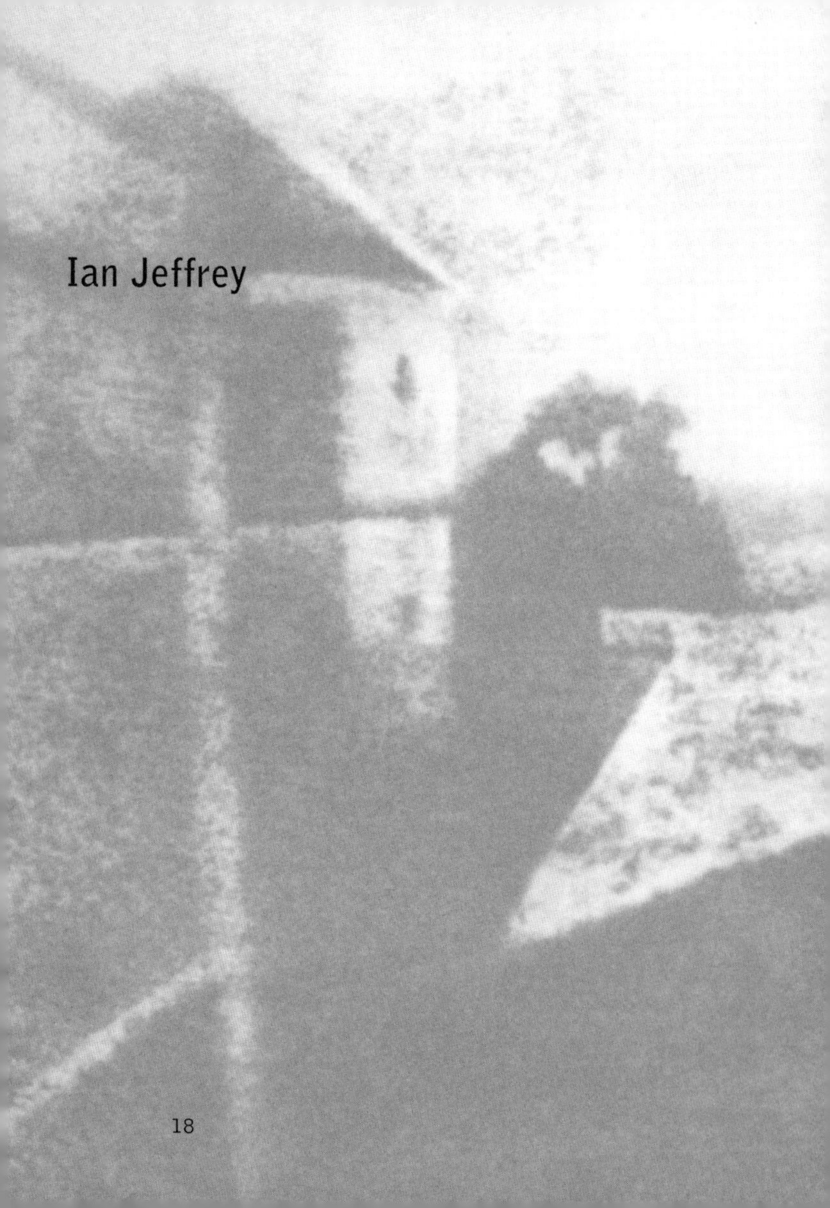

Ian Jeffrey

What has been done, a true history of photography or just a sort of archeology?

Most photo-history lies somewhere between archaeology and chronicling. By 'a true history' I imagine that you mean an account written by someone in possession of an ideological certainty. There are histories of that kind but they belong rather to the history of thought. For the last half century or so, historians have been called on to write histories of photography dating back to the beginning and concluding at the present moment. This has resulted in an abbreviated, hurried kind of narration, which makes no more than a decent minimum of reference to aesthetics and technicalities. Any writer in the empirical camp is only too well aware of what has been left out, principally because it is beyond the mental grasp of most researchers: an informed history of colour photography is the most notable example. But to return to 'the truth', which can't simply be dismissed as a vacuous piety. The truth, in this context, has a metaphysical dimension and it is always on hand inviting formulation. The empiricist, for example, will be able to give you the exact details of the introduction of the Leica during the 1920s; and that is a satisfying story, often retold, but it is far from sufficient. I have noticed that the small horizontal format, exemplified by the Leica, began to be used by German amateur military photographers at around the time of Verdun (1916). I guess that there was a craving at the time for the sort of informal, continuous, non-hieratic picture, which became associated with the name Leica. By now I am beginning to connect that particular aesthetic, which we think of as synonymous with modernism, with the mentality of a German soldier faced by the likelihood of death and glory in the spring of 1916. So I might just as well read Ernst Jünger and E.M. Remarque if I am to understand the onset of the new miniature format and its aesthetic. Photography history has not concerned itself very much with this underlying truth, or truth of the spirit. Many of us have been happy enough to take a Foucauldian view, assuming a manipulative authority intent on maintaining itself. My view is that photography, despite its potential for surveillance and management, has been above all a vernacular art medium, responsive to shifts in the popular mood. The idea of 'a popular mood' is, of course, controversial, for it has Jüngian and mystical undertones, as if we, or groups of us, unknowingly evolved turns of mind in unison. You must remember, however, that photography, since the introduction of 'detective' and lightweight cameras in the 1880s and 1890s, has been increasingly subject to spontaneous use. A true history of the medium entails a theory of the collective unconscious. More cautiously, you might say that you could well consider such a theory via the history of photography.

Beaumont Newhall: his approach and its shortcomings

Newhall's *The History of Photography* first came out in 1937, and it was substantially written in 1949. It is the work of a liberal historian: a believer that is to say, in the primacy of individual innovators and artists. Helmut and Alison Gernsheim's great book of 1955, also called *The History of Photography*, is another such liberal enterprise, determined to give credit to worthy individuals. Historians of that era were fixated on an idea of (name) recognition for effort and ingenuity. History of this liberal kind was a sifting process whereby artists of talent gained access to the Pantheon, or to its contemporary equivalent – the museum collection. Newhall's book was written for M.O.M.A., in New York., and it was the first in a long line of important surveys sponsored by museums. Inevitably this has skewed history writing towards certifiable product, attributed pieces –if possible by Gustave le Gray or Roger Fenton. But is there anything wrong with such liberal history? It is premised on an idea of transparency. Prolonged study of artist X will uncover the exact circumstances in which the work was produced, for whom and for what reason. Even though this degree of clarity is rarely achieved, especially in photography, liberal historians like to believe that the truth can be laid hold of once and for all. By now we know that this aspiration towards full disclosure is a fantasy or at best unattainable. We may also be bored by it, aware that it no longer interests us.

History is written, as often as not, in response to a contemporary predicament. Now we are post-modernists, participating in a continuous and integrated cultural process. Modernists, such as Newhall and Gernsheim, took it for granted that the artwork was a discrete element with a transcendental and long-term validity. Art in the modern era involved transactions between individuals, between Duchamp and his patrons, between Walker Evans and Lincoln Kirstein. Art in the post-modern era features an enigmatic public, represented by a range of agents and middlemen: curators, journalists, dealers – some in tune with the public, and some not. Artists produce for this inscrutable audience. Art takes its place with popular music, sport and 'news', and has to be thought of in relation to the culture of entertainment and distraction. Authentic post-modern product doesn't keep, in the way that a modernist piece might. A Warhol item, for example, belongs irrevocably to a particular cultural moment increasingly beyond recall. A picture by Edward Weston, on the other hand, outlives its cultural moment and never properly belonged to it in the first place. This situation has relevance to the practice of photohistory. The post-modern predicament, with respect to 'the public', was rehearsed by stereo-photographers in the 1850s and 1860s. And the first great puzzled seeker after a public was the inventor himself, Fox Talbot in the 1840s. Experience of the cultural situation now means that one looks, almost instinctively, for precursor moments. I find them in the stereo age with its sometimes crazy quest for audiences, and in the incredibly variable and uncertain art of Fox Talbot.

Which are the main trends (cultural, ideological, and political) that have ruled the dominant historiographic models?

Traditional history, best exemplified by Newhall and Gernsheim, held to the idea that history was the work of individuals. This liberal idea took such a firm hold because photography, until 1910 or so, was a practice centred on learned societies, enthusiastic annalists of their own achievements. Until the arrival of the big industrial-scientific conglomerates around 1910, spearheaded by the Lumières who developed the Authochrome process, most artistic and scientific achievements could be attributed to named workers (as they were called in the journals). Thus the idea of photography as an autonomous practice took hold. However, it became increasingly evident during the twentieth century that photography had become as all-pervading as writing and print culture. A history that took this into account would be impossibly broad. At the same time it couldn't be denied that photography was any longer the delimited practice it once had been. Historians in the 1970s tried to take account of the new persuasiveness of photography by drawing on the work of the French theorists, Foucault and Lacan in particular. Foucault, with his interests in management and surveillance, stimulated attention to photographic recording, with respect to prisoners and marginals. Unfortunately, the new historians were more devoted to their theory sources than they were to the material in question. The result was a macaronic writing, splintered by attention to an excess of sanctified theoretical texts. All the same, the determination to broaden the scope of photographic studies was admirable.

The most determined attempt to escape from the post-modern morass was made by Mike Weaver, author of *The Photographic Art* (1986). Weaver's tactic was to deal only with those photographers who could be thought of as artists… all the rest was sociology. There are many interesting difficulties involved in Weaver's approach to history. How are artist-photographers to be identified? On their own say-so, or by the historian critic? Photography is also, as anyone will admit, rich in unselfconscious artists. Weaver's way around this problem is to identify a tradition of icons and formats to which the photographer-artist appears to have an intuitive access. To a post-modernist, of course, Weaver's ideas are intolerable, because they are premised on hierarchy and on a distinction, valid at all times, between art and non-art. This, however, has always been a distinction difficult to make with respect to photography, and one of the reasons why we are so fascinated by the medium.

Can Photography be considered an autonomous discipline or would it be more useful to analyse its applications in other fields, such as journalism, advertising, and anthropology?

Certainly, other fields exist. The problem, however, is that not all of these other fields are of equal importance. It seems to me that one history of photography ought to involve all those moments when what you might call secular photography impinges on the imagination of an age. Fashion photography, for instance, seems always to have been with us, but I would have to be convinced of its importance; and likewise with advertising. 'Other fields' only seem to become interesting when their product is in excess of its context. A new mode might be developed to fill a minor role, but it turns out to have an unexpected supplementary value: photomicrography in the 1850s is a good instance of this, as is snapshot photography in the 1890s. There are a number of tentative developments which seem significant far in excess of their ostensible importance: the panoramic format introduced by Kodak in the 1890s, and colour as it was developed in the years just before the Great War. One of the most important of these 'other fields' was celestial photography, from 1880s onwards; it infiltrated a new concept of the sublime into public consciousness. One aspect of the kind of developments, which I have listed, is that they caused uncertainty and even disquiet. Snapshots, for instance, introduced their first exponents to figures so vacuous and remote that they were intolerable. Autochromes, with their emphasis on the sentient world, implied a humanity so hedonistic as to be blameworthy. Kodak's popular panoramic cameras of the 1890s represented the world (streets usually) so even-handedly and dispassionately as to call all sense of hierarchy into question. Even the Leica and 35mm photography as it evolved in the 1920s laid a disproportionate emphasis on private experience, for many Leica pictures in the beginning were contact printed and could only be accessed by glass. That is, not all photography's contributions have been reassuring to the establishment, to the state, to the smooth management of affairs. Any comprehensive history of the medium ought to concern itself with such moments of destabilisation as I have mentioned.

What should be more relevant, a history of artists or a history of images?
The phrase 'a history of images' implies, if I understand it correctly, that there is an identifiable mood or mentality which craves and recognises a certain sort of imagery, and which passes on when the craving is satisfied. Vietnam in the 1960s produced two such images: that of the burned child running down the road, and that of the Loan execution of the man in a checked shirt. Or you might nominate some of the Moonwalk pictures. To go further back; the French in the 1940s were drawn to Nadar's portraits of artists and musicians, embodiments of an inherent cultural distinction. Anyone writing 'a history of images' would have to consider the question of group mentality. Is it manipulated into being, or is it somehow spontaneous? One problem with 'a history of images' (understood as iconic, resonant images) is that it ought to be restricted to eras characterised by a public mobilised and subject to a regime of images. As far as I am aware, those conditions only obtained in the modern era, from the 1920s through into the 1960s. Afterwards the media became profuse and de-centred. Only the modernists believed

in the primacy of the single, cathartic image, of the kind achieved by
H. Cartier-Bresson and by A. Kertész (and achieved by them only for
a relatively short period in the 1930s). In late- and post-modernism the norm is a continuum of images, moving from one inconclusive moment to the next – as we see for the first time and most
convincingly in R. Frank's *The Americans* (1958).

On the other hand, by 'a history of images' you may mean a history
of pictorial types: the full-body portrait style one sees in A. Sander's
pictures, for example, or the powdered mask-like faces typical of
Berlin modernism in the late 1920s. Genealogical work of this kind
is irresistible. It casts the historian as a forensic expert on the track
of originating moments. In truth such originating moments are
slippery and hopelessly elusive, but one knows that they must have
existed, even if unrecognised by their hosts. You are dealing here with
something like the philosopher's stone of photo-history, with a certainty, which can never really be nailed. Better perhaps to stick with
prime instances of the type or format and to say that it was at its
peak in 1932 or in '56. Any 'history of images' is beset by such black
holes in the research map.

As I said, with respect to 'a history of artists', we don't rightly know
who the artists are. It is more than likely that the real artist will turn
out to be a village portraitist practising above a bicycle shop… I am
thinking of Jacob Molenhuis, the Dutchman (1894-1987), or Disfarmer or Bellocq, or some other operative who had nothing more
than an all-important knack of getting the man or woman in the
street to present him or herself as never before. Another major difficulty with 'a history of artists' is that photographers, unlike painters,

tend to peak briefly, never regaining the heights. This implies that any history of artists cannot be disengaged from the broader history of culture, and that the great modernist photographers at least practised in the closest possible contact with their cultural moment…. virtually as creatures of the culture.

Is social history compatible with aesthetic history, and a history of uses with a history of forms?

The two histories are inter-dependent. Take modernism, as represented by E. Weston and H. Cartier-Bresson. Theirs was the era of the Leica, and of widespread popular camera ownership, an era of the over-production of imperfectly registered banalities… an aesthetic trough. It is difficult to understand the great photographic art of that period without taking into account the huge hinterland of production, which served as a background. Modernism was a redemptive enterprise, a search for the cathartic image, which would transcend and dissolve all the rest. It is possible that art photography since the 1920s has always been meant to contradict the platitudes of mass production.

W. Benjamin stated that we should rethink photography and history altogether, because what transforms an event into an historical event is its technical reproductability.

Benjamin was, of course, speaking from the point of view of the 1930s when the authorities in Germany were becoming aware of the uses of publicity, at a time when events were beginning to be staged for the benefit of the camera. This was certainly not true of the 1914-

18 war when the camera was no more than tolerated by rulers and military celebrities. The Kaiser, Chancellor Bethmann-Hollweg and others were it seems incapable of seeing beyond those physically present. Their successors in the 1930s were the first to be able to envisage the mass elsewhere as the audience and the present as a stage. The gist of Benjamin's assertion is that if an event didn't take place in front of the camera it might as well not have taken place at all. Conversely, any major public and political event photographed in the modern age is inherently unbelievable. What this has resulted in has been a craving for the authentic. Dissatisfied with a diet of state appearances, audiences have desired what can be believed in, and thus photo-reportage in particular has constantly renewed itself. It ought to be added that Benjamin's diagnosis doesn't extend to the liberal democracies where the state is not alone in determining 'historical events'. The Vietnam War, for instance, was characterised by many recorded events, which the state would have preferred to keep off the stage of history. If Benjamin's proposition still applies it does so with respect to T.V., which charts and mediates history for the bulk of the electorate. Photography, in this context, has become a supplementary medium, one, which draws attention and fills in the details overlooked by T.V. This secondary situation in the world of news-gathering has become one of the subjects of photo-reportage: Peress's exceptional *Telex Persan* of 1984 is precisely about the photographer's distance from *events*.

Ian Jeffrey, is a historian and author of, among other books, *Revisions: An alternative History of Photography*.

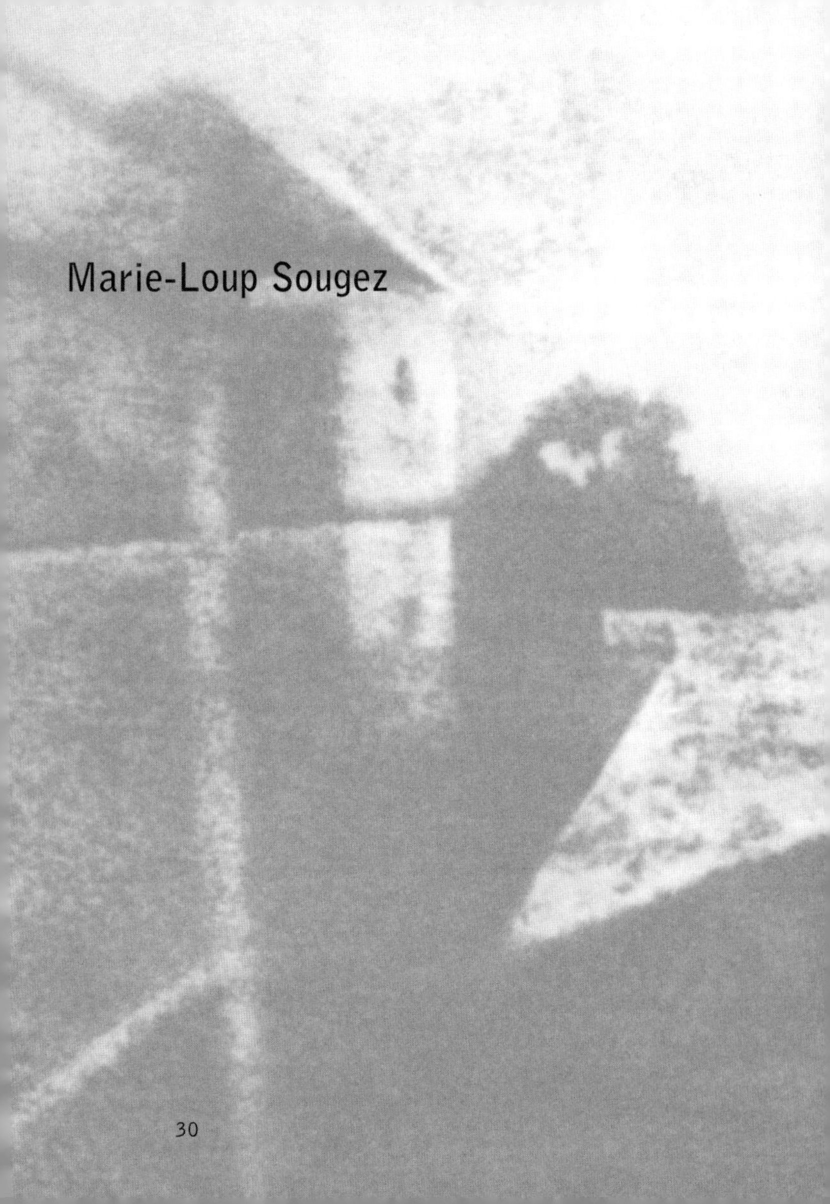

Marie-Loup Sougez

It is far from easy to put forward alternatives to the history of photography as this has been written up until now, all the more so when one has, even if only to a small extent, contributed to it. Obviously, however, the currently existing models, regarded at this end of the century, do not seem very satisfying to me.

First, I will attempt to draw up a balance of the publications at our disposal up to the present time, touching in passing on the deficiencies and repetitions of the existing material and at the same time excusing to some extent the shortcomings of this body of material. I will then go on to propose some alternatives that seem to me to be desirable, but founding these proposals on the specific idiosyncrasies of photography itself, which in my view have not been considered with the necessary thoroughness.

Prior to the history by Beaumont Newhall, basically what we had was the one by Josef Maria Eder (*Geschichte der Photographie*, 1890, with subsequent German editions and an English translation). This history was clearly written from a technique-oriented point of view and with an undeniable German bias in the selection of the names of inventors and photographers. In due course the history by Georges Potonniée (*Histoire de la Découverte de la Photographie*, 1925) focused on the reconstruction of the early days of the medium in France, taking a stand in favour of Niépce and Bayard, undermining the importance of Daguerre and playing down the decisive role of Fox Talbot.

A few years later there appeared the first text by Beaumont Newhall, initially published on the occasion of the great retrospective exhibition organised by the MoMA (*Photography 1839-1937: A Short*

Critical History, 1937), afterwards extended and successively reprinted (*History of Photography from 1839 to the Present Day*, 1949; Spanish edition published in 1983).

Bearing in mind the date of its first publication, I do not consider the basic approach adopted by Beaumont Newhall's history especially open to criticism for the fact of being based on the history of a technique. Indeed, Newhall was the first to take account of the creative contribution made largely by Europe after the First World War, a period of great richness from which the United States was soon to benefit with the massive influx of photographers fleeing Nazi persecution. Newhall's was the first history to include futurists, Constructivists and Dadaists. However, apart from the pages he devoted to photojournalism, he did not deal with the whole spectrum of photography and he was the first to draw the line –with a solid methodological framework from which we can still benefit today– that was to mark all of the subsequent histories, but with a deliberate emphasis on the USA that ignores the work of non-American photographers.

The deficiencies I find in Newhall's approach are due precisely to the neglect of those other, non-artistic aspects that were to be reflected in the work of Raymond Lécuyer (*Histoire de la Photographie*, 1945), although Lécuyer does indeed manifest a pronounced chauvinism and a conservative and even outmoded aesthetics. This has contributed to the fact that the important data contained in Lécuyer's book, concerning a whole range of applications, mainly in relation to the mechanical means of reproduction, the crucial stimulus for new developments in photography, did not receive its due share of attention.

The later histories —namely the one by Helmut and Alison Gernsheim (*The History of Photography from the Earliest Use of the Camera Obscura to the Beginning of the Modern Era,* 1955) and the subsequent publications of these authors and the history by Noemi Rosenblum (*A World History of Photography,* 1984), all with an evident bias towards English-speaking photographers, do not move very far from Newhall's approach. The Gernsheims' does not go beyond the early years of the 20th century, and Rosenblum attaches more importance to documentary photography and photojournalism.

Taking these models as their basis, many of the later works approach the study of the medium as if it were archaeology. On very few occasions has a real history of photography been written, and in the majority of cases what we have are hybrid works which combine the archaeological aspect (referring to the origins of the medium and its subsequent development up to the start of the 20th century) with more or less reliable addenda dealing with contemporary works which often cover only the most recent work on the basis of criteria that have more to do with current fashions and the art market than with a genuine vision of the medium as a whole. In the last few years there has been an increasing emphasis on the contribution made by photography to the historic avant-garde, as well as on the new resources that those movements found in photography, and this makes it possible to build a bridge between painterly aesthetics and present-day photographic works, something that was hardly conceivable for a considerable number of years.

For some time now certain historians and art critics have been taking an interest in photography. However, with the exception of certain indispensable studies such as the essays of Rosalind E. Krauss (*The originality of the avant-garde and other modern myths*), it seems to me that in many cases they have falsified the discourse through a failure to understand the medium in depth, and this has increased the tendency to take only creative photography into account (with fervent opposition from the defenders of the documentary or informative school). As a result, when the avowed purpose is to draw together the different aspects of photography into a panoramic vision, the enterprise breaks down where it touches on other facets of the medium and has evident difficulty in treating the whole with impartiality.

To come back to the question of the archaeological treatment of the beginnings of photography, I think that at the time when the principal extant histories were commenced such a treatment was inevitable. Although the data here are from a relatively recent period, the historian is confronted with serious gaps in the picture which oblige us to dig down into a past that is close in time but arduous of access. A further difficulty is that we do not have the necessary distance to evaluate the role of photography and its numerous applications.

To go back to what I noted above about the nationalist character of the majority of the existing texts, the question arises here of the cultural, ideological, religious and political filters that have conditioned the main models available to us. Of course, these filters are present in many other fields, but it would seem that photography, because it is a relatively recent medium in historical terms, evidences in a more blatantly frontal manner the allegiances of those who write its history. The treatment given to the photographic nude has been beset with innumerable difficulties, and continues to be the object of suspicions and misgivings. This is no more than a reflection offered in passing, as an indication of the multiple filters from which photography is still suffering, when for a long time now other art forms have been allowed to express themselves freely. While it is true that these filters are highly apparent, it seems to me that the national or cultural supremacies (and, of course, their counterparts in religion, too) are the ones which most severely encumber the areas they cover.

Although they are slowly opening up to an acceptance of foreign works, the recent texts still show a blatant lack of balance between the attention given to the work of photographers from the author's own country (or from his most immediate cultural environment) and those from other parts of the world, of which only the most outstanding figures are dealt with. At times, too, in a display of ecumenical openness, it comes about that minor works of exotic origin are cited more or less at random as a concession to the claims of the Third World, dismissing the whole issue without any kind of scholarly criteria or in depth study.

Allow me to insist yet again here on something we have already noted, namely the need to go back to the very origins of photography, to what was its *raison d'être* for those who were its first pioneers. These were driven not by commercial motives but by that 19th-century enthusiasm for the practice of new techniques with a basis in science that pointed in the direction of extending knowledge, although they were often influenced, too, by national interests and monopolistic policies, it has to be said.

Photography emerged as a *mechanical* means of reproduction with the development of the illustrated book and the picture press and the dissemination of knowledge of all kinds. An instrument ideally suited to the great blossoming of archaeological research, to travel, and to the first systematic attempts to catalogue the world's artistic and monumental treasures and to make known the holdings of the great museums. This is another aspect of the greatest importance which is increasingly being taken into account.

These issues were first addressed, in a very effective manner, by Walter Benjamin and Gisèle Freund. We are also indebted to them for their study of the sociological impact of photography, its role in making the possession of a portrait accessible to all, as well as in bringing the masses into contact with all kinds of knowledge. Benjamin was the first to insist on the issue of the social implications of the reproducibility of the image. A highly topical question nowadays, when so many photographers, encouraged by a market dominated by gallery owners and dealers, are involved in producing works in numbered series, and sometimes even one-off works, certifying the non-use or even the destruction of the original negative.

But to come back to the key question of the present survey —namely, what is to be the new model for the history of photography— I think it is essential to insist on the fact that when we talk about photography, we are talking about an autonomous and Protean discipline. While the photograph can now be found among the most highly valued works on the art market, it is often no more than just another instrument, ranked among the so-called mixed techniques, which seems justified to me although I think it is a long way from many other aspects of photography *per se*. In fact, photography as one technique among the many used by creative artists is not a matter of great importance among. Far more important is the fundamental role of photography in the development of the avant-garde movements of the 20th century and the visual impact it had on the artists of the 19th century. The Spanish translation of Aaron Scharf's book *Art and Photography* (*Arte y fotografía*, 1994) was a long time coming, in that the first edition in English dates from 1968. (I merely mention this circumstance in passing before going back to the question that concerns us).

Photography is an autonomous discipline, the technical nature of which must not be neglected when in any study of its history. Not as a detailed study of formulas and optical calculations, but taking account of the multiplicity of its applications in a great variety of fields. Nor should we forget its original *raison d'être*: the reproducibility of the image. But this in no sense prevents its being considered in terms of certain specific sectors, ranging from a purely technical and professional application to much broader fields such as art or anthropology.

What of the approaches should prevail, a history of photographers or a history of a images? For me, we are dealing fundamentally with a history of images because — in addition to a great personal enjoyment of the iconographic vision — I think this is the best way to educate the eye and to learn to see the world photographically. But I also believe that this urge for visual bombardment does not come into conflict with knowing about the photographers who created those images, being familiar with their cultural environment, the way they lived, their interests, the ideology that inspired them, etc. All of that makes it possible to follow the evolution of a particular photographer, his association with this tendency or that, and in so doing to structure our general understanding of the most diverse movements, which very often (and above all in the first half of the 20th century) overlap in quite unexpected ways.

At the same time, I believe that an aesthetic history and a social history are compatible with one another, just as in due course — although I do not see this as so imperative — a history of uses can be combined with a history of forms. More and more attention is now being given to the photography of the unknown amateur, holiday snaps and the family album. Because I am convinced that photography is a medium with a character of its own and one that requires its own individual treatment. It is not a matter of confining photography in a ghetto but of recognizing its particularity. This is why it proves so difficult to link it with art history, an undertaking which has to date been less than satisfactory.

Tacking on photography as an additional subject in the study of art history would, in my opinion, be rather like including cinema in the history of theatre. The incorporation of the history of photography into the university syllabus is an extremely complex issue, and one which needs to be looked into very seriously, and soon. In all honesty, I am not at all sure how it can be incorporated in a satisfactory way. When it comes to addressing this issue seriously in Spain we can, of course, turn to the models already in use, basically in the United States, but also in various European countries.

When designing study programmes in Spain it seems to me to be very important to reflect on what has been happening here over the last twenty years. After being quite without any history of its own, Spanish photography has seen the flourishing of a considerable number of studies devoted to recovering the photographic legacy in terms of a town or city, an Autonomous Region or the state as a whole. In many cases this has led to a certain navel-gazing localism, and to situations where the local photographer of some remote village is ranked alongside the most important figures of international photography. I hope these remarks will not be misinterpreted: I am very far from wishing to cast doubt on the importance of the research carried out all over the Iberian Peninsula (having mentioned the Peninsula, it occurs to me to wonder what we know about Portuguese photography). I simply want to plead, insistently, that the conditions are created here to train researchers who will also take an interest in international photography, in order that a discipline with a balanced spread of knowledge can be taught.

Spanish universities already have a fair number of post-doctoral and Ph.D. students whose theses are centred on photography. From them we can look forward to the emergence of a staff body that will be capable of teaching those aspects that are still lacking. In fact there are already some instances of this, but these individuals find themselves unable to develop with the necessary freedom in the absence of a suitably designed programme.

This multifaceted aspect of photography to which I have been referring before calls for an approach that cannot be the work of any one author alone. The courageous but insufficient effort of the *Histoire de la Photographie* (1986), under the direction of Jean-Claude Lemagny and André Rouillé, has been considerably extended by the *Nouvelle Histoire de la Photographie* (1994), under the supervision of Michel Frizot. I believe that this is the direction we have to go in. At the same time, the idea of establishing a world-wide history that provides a space for minorities, marginal and Third World photographers strikes me as rather difficult to achieve. Every time an attempt of this kind has been made in the past it has proved to be no more than a mere gesture and, in most cases, prompted by a sense of obligation and wholly lacking in the necessary rigour. The idea of putting together a global history of photography can only be carried through on the basis of a study carried out by a series of writers specialised in particular areas, oriented towards the compilation of a great conjoint work that would take account of the different periods and facets of the medium as well as the various geographical areas and socio-cultural contexts.

The different histories of countries or particular geographical or cultural areas can at time provide us with valuable insights that would be worth drawing in to this ideal complete history. What will be difficult will be to give each part a balanced treatment in order to produce something homogeneous.

Has anyone yet attempted a comparable undertaking in relation to cinema, music, literature or painting? Let us hope that photography may be a pioneer in this type of global study.

Sougez, Marie-Loup is a historian and essayist.

FROM THE "NEWHALL SCHOOL" TO THE "HISTORIES" OF PHOTOGRAPHY: EXPERIENCES AND PROPOSALS FOR THE FUTURE

Bernardo Riego

There is a certain bashfulness that overcomes any historian when he or she has to explain how a work of historiography is constructed. The task of interpreting the historical fact is, ultimately, a process of communication with the reader in which aspects of the past are brought to light in line with a method of actuation that seeks to answer a series of questions which the historian asked herself in those first moments when she began to take an interest in a certain theme. How was photography introduced into Spain? Who were the members, and what work was produced by, this or that aesthetic group? What were the debates generated by photography in the 19th-century? Etc., etc. Behind any historical text there is a series of questions initial, and behind those questions there is a historian with an acquired knowledge and a series of *a priori* assumptions, who explores a situation, gathers information, and fashions out of the chaos of documents that come to her attention a coherent explanation which she places at the disposal of her audience. The outcome of her work is never neutral, but takes place inside a conceptual frame of analysis that reflects both the background of the author and the time in which the work was produced. Of course, Borges illuminated this latter aspect with masterly irony in his short story "Pierre Menard, author of the Quixote" showing us a 20th-century "author" who, in "rewriting" (or more exactly, copying) the work of Cervantes, was in fact disseminating values that belonged to the 17th century and were clearly anachronistic and unexpected in his time. Something similar happens to the historian, who needs to be aware that she is disseminating knowledge for her time and utilizing, even when she does not make not this explicit, cultural values which are in vigour when her work was produced.

These guidelines are valid not only for general history, but also for the various specialized histories, and the history of photography can be inscribed within this sub-genre. In fact, in the English-speaking world the preferred usage is quite emphatically not "the History of Photography", but "Histories". For example, Anne McCauley[1] (1997, 88) distinguishes between: "Histories [of Photography] which were in fact disguised debates on the priority of the invention; Histories as handbooks, and Histories of the photographic image". In the first case she offers examples such as the foundational book by Daguerre, and for the handbooks, works such as those by Josef Maria Eder or Pottonié. It is a way of classifying a historiography which, like the position of photography itself, has always been complex, and which changed the object of its study in the course of the 19th and 20th centuries.

In two earlier works, (Riego, 1994 and 1996)[2] and before coming to address the issue of photographic historiography as this has manifested itself in the Spanish state before and after 1981, I undertook a gen-

1 Anne MacCauley: 1997. "Writing photography's History before Newhall." In: *History of Photography, Why Historiography?*. Volume 21. N° 2. 1997. pp. 88-101.

2 Bernardo Riego: – 1994. "De la 'Fotohistoria' a la Historia con la Fotografía" In: *Fotografia y Metodos Históricos: dos textos para un debate*. Universidad de Cantabria/Universidad de La Laguna. Santander/Santa Cruz de Tenerife 1994. pp. 11-37. (Text in Spanish).

– 1996. "La historiografía española y los debates sobre la Fotografía como fuente histórica", in *Ayer* N° 24. Mario P. Diaz Barrado, (Editor) Madrid 1996. pp. 91-111. – 1999. "Imágenes Fotográficas y estrategias de opinión pública: Los viajes de la Reina Isabel II por España (1858-1866)" In *Reales Sitios. Monográfico sobre Historia de la Fotografía*. Patrimonio Nacional. Madrid 1999. pp. 2-13.

eral synthesis of the way in which the History of Photography had evolved on the international plane. While in the 19th century photography was conceived of as a derivative of science and technology and its development was explained from that premiss, in the 20th century, starting with the work of Beaumont Newhall, the historical object changed radically, and came to privilege the study of the photographers and the images they had produced, inscribing these in a technical periodization that is suspiciously reminiscent of those found in the methodology of the history of art (Newhall's own academic background was in this discipline) even when their analyses make use of a differentiated terminology. Eder and Newhall would thus be the supreme exponents of two different historiographic visions of photography, the key elements of which would be the positivist conception of history in Eder's case, and the pursuit of historiographic utility in the service of the great collections in the case of Newhall and his followers, who have survived up to the present, at a time when this school of historical interpretation has fulfilled its objective, is clearly exhausted, and its considerable conceptual shortcomings are more and more openly apparent.

It is not my intention to repeat in the present text arguments I have already presented in earlier works, to which I refer those readers who may be interested in them. It seems to me to be more appropriate to take this opportunity to attempt an analysis of the current situation and to put forward proposals for historical research in various directions and to respond in this way to the challenges presented to us by our own time. As a historian, during the first years in which I published on photography, from 1981 on, I numbered myself among the ranks of the photo-historians, faithful to the models of the Newhall school, so fragmentarily received in Spain. In the course of the nineties I started to explore new historiographic paths, having discovered, through my work in the University, that the parameters of analysis being proposed by this model led only to the creation of an interminable *pantheon of photographers,* to endowing 19th-century works with a present *artistic quality,* in which sense they clearly served the interests of the international collectors. (In due course I will refer to the recent Clifford case, which seems to me to be a very clear example) and, above all, to construct a history that functioned as a satellite of the more consolidated national photographic historiographies. The confirmation that in the early eighties, when a modern Spanish photographic historiography was starting to develop, we had been subscribing to a moribund school, came to me from the European conferences I attended in the course of that decade in various international settings. What was being asked of Spanish historians at that time was that we provide new names for the universal pantheon, that we confirm the importance of the French or British influence in this country, (I shall also refer below to the writing of nationalist photographic history) and that no importance was attached to the ideological or cultural aspects which in effect determined the very existence of photography as such and endowed it with its true importance, over and above national particularities.

I recall that in 1996, in Charleroi, I put forward a view of how Spanish intellectuals regarded photography in the 19th century. I set out from the premiss that, just as nowadays many intellectuals are aware of *virtual reality* as a technology and seek to gauge its cultural importance even although they have no direct contact with it, in the 19th century, photography, for all the various differences, was in a similar situation. Its very existence implied a series of values to which the intellectuals of the moment responded with pride, but which were dissociated from the practice of the photographers themselves. It was a matter of evidencing the cultural importance of a technology that was delivering social responses at a time when it was expanding its scope with great efficacy. I discovered with a certain chagrin that, except for a small minority, what interested the great majority of those present was the question of the predominance of French-speaking over English-speaking photographers, or vice versa. In that model there was no room for historians from the fringes of Europe, be they Spanish, Scandinavian or whatever, who were concerned with the cultural, social or ideological values of the space constructed by photography in its historical evolution.

I would like to address some of the characteristics of that photographic historiography which derives from the models created by the Newhall school and its European followers, and which is still widely practised even now. In one sense, this is a *decontextualized* history of the cultural, social, economic and political phenomena within which the actual production of photographic images is inscribed. What is important is the *photographers,* while essential aspects of their work are ignored; aspects such as the *intentionality,* the *institutional chain* (who commissions the images and for what purpose, how they are disseminated, etc.,) and the *frame of cultural reception* which makes possible the legibility of those images at the moment when they are placed in circulation. There is a homogenizing of the *artistic quality* of the photographers, something which in the 19th century is in many cases highly questionable (Bill Jay, 1991)[3], and any influences external to the photography itself are ignored, the result of this being an *autarchic,* suspicious and at times pessimistic vision, (Rouille et al., 1995)[4] which means in consequence that specialists from other cultural fields external to that of photography fail to encounter elements of contact between this historiography and their areas of interest even when these are addressed with rigour and ability. There is thus a *short-circuiting* of one of the essential characteristics of intellectual production, that of the *participation in* and *exchange of* the results obtained. What is promoted is a *nationalist historiographic vision,* one which has, for example, reduced debates such as the one concerning invention to a contest between the French and the British. (Niece and Dagger *versus* Talbot). How is it possible, in such a reductionist context, to explain the fact of different researchers in different parts of the world working on that same idea at more or less the same time? It is obvious that the recourse to a nationalist historiography, in which the differences between the British and the French, was already present form the very outset (Riego, 1996); an approach which was to be replicated in the Germany of the National Socialist era, in the work of Erich Stenger, but one which in the present day and age serves only to obscure from view the far richer reality of the intercultural role played by photography, both in its technological identity and in its contribution to the construction of a graphic imaginary after 1839, as a response to the needs of a society engaged in re-articulating its vision of the world, a function which Walter Benjamin elucidated with great subtlety seventy or so years ago.

3 Bill Jay: 1991. *Cyanide & Spirits An Inside-Out View of Early Photography.* Nazraeli Press. Munich 1991.
4 André Rouille et al. 1995 "La photographie, est-elle une image pauvre?". Monograph in *La Recherche photographique.* N° 18. Paris 1995.

Another of the singular characteristics of this model of historiography consists in the need to create *mythic photographers* who are consolidated as fundamental within that *pantheon* that gives chronological continuity to the interpretation of a coherent evolution of photographic artists from 1839 up until the present. The aim here was to create a roster of photographers capable of satisfying the categories of periodization embodied in the model. This amounted to an international hall of fame which, as is well known, was created on the basis of the photographers represented in the personal collections of the first historians of this school (Gernsheim, for example), into which the subsequently *discovered* new names were duly incorporated. This is a mechanism which has served at the same time to re-evaluate the major public and private collections through the putting into circulation of new historic photographers who are endowed with a "presentist" artistic value, even when the analysis of the historical documents reveals divergencies with respect to the photographers' perceptions of their own works or the conditions of their production. With regard to Spain we have recently witnessed the *case* of Charles Clifford, a photographer of British origin who worked from an early date for the government of Queen Isabel II (by way of the Ministerio de Fomento), for the Spanish Crown itself, and for one or two national illustrated magazines, as a figure who in terms of the interests North American collections satisfied the requisites for entering into the *historical pantheon* as a representative of 19th-century Spanish photography. Among the points in this photographer's favour were his British background and the fact that a significant part of his output had already been exported to the United States, and to a lesser extent to the rest of Europe, effectively exploiting the manifest lack of interest on the part of Spain's cultural authorities in protecting the country's photographic heritage. The process of international re-evaluation was glaringly evident when the Spanish Ministerio de Educación y Cultura itself organized an anthological exhibition of this photographer's work in Madrid, in which the images selected by the commissioner were for the most part copies on loan from public and private collections in North America, in spite of that fact that it would have been far less expensive to use other copies of the same images in the possession of Spanish institutions; that, however, would not have produced the effect that was really being sought, and which can be appreciated with absolute clarity in the approach manifested in the catalogue (Fontanella, 1996)[5]. Although I have since attempted, in the wake of this exhibition, to superimpose an alternative historiographic vision of Clifford, one which does not in any way seek to dispute the work's aesthetic quality but does ponder the conditions of its production, (Riego, 1999), the fact is that the construction of the Clifford myth (like so many instances of the fringe countries' cultural output) is concerned not with representing 19th-century Spanish photography in the annals of international, but with raising the value of the already established collections of this photographer's work. Every historian of the 19th century is familiar with many other Spanish photographers whose work is of an interest and a quality at least as great as Charles Clifford's, but who did not have the "good fortune" to be English-speaking.

5 Lee Fontanella: 1996. Charles Clifford. *Fotógrafo de la España de Isabel II*. Ministerio de Educación y Cultura. Ediciones el Viso. Madrid 1996.

It would, however, be unjust not to enumerate here the contributions made by the Newhall school to the cultural valorization of photography. When a historiographic model has consolidated itself and been in force for so long a period of time, it is evident that the strength of its must be explained by its having managed to provide an effective response to certain perceived needs. History has functions that are explicit, and others that are implicit, to which I will refer at the end of this text. During the thirties the change of historical object with regard to photography, which as we have already seen effectively shifted its attention from technical developments to the images themselves, had an immediate impact on the policies of those public institutions which already had photographs in their collections. From occupying a place of secondary importance within the institution, these came to form part of the principal holdings. A particularly well-studied case is that of the Victoria and Albert Museum in London, whose photographic collection was originally seen as purely functional, but with this change of historical object brought about by means of the Newhall school, the functional gave way to the artistic. (González Vallejo, 1998)[6]. The archive and the museum have created a new space for the organization of images, (Sekulla, 1991, Crimp, 1995)[7,8] but in addition to their indisputable role of diffusion and cultural valorization, they have also stim-

6 Vicente González Vallejo, : Photographing the Museum: Photographs in the early years of the Victorian and Albert Museum, University of Leicester, 1998. (unpublished)
7 Alan Sekulla: 1991. "Reading an Archive" In: *Blasted Allegories*. Brian Wallis, Marcia Tucker (Eds.) MIT Press 1991.
8 Douglas Crimp: *On the Museum's Ruins*, Cambrigde, MIT Press, 1995.

ulated the formation of a body of specialists in the conservation and restoration of photographs and the emergence of a tradition of research in the field of these media and their conservation, giving rise to the paradox that there are now very few types of museum holdings which have the backing of so much technical knowledge as do the photographic media. Nor should we overlook, among the achievements of the Newhall school, the fact that the assimilation of historic photographs to the status of other artistic genres has generated an international market which manifests itself in auctions and in the acquisition of those photographic images that have a place in that pantheon to which we referred above, although one of the secondary consequences of this is that any photographic work with an artistic intention is liable to be drawn into the market and assigned an economic value. Nevertheless, we should not forget that this market reveals asymmetries between the United States and the countries of southern Europe, Latin America and elsewhere; places which, on account of this asymmetry, are occasionally exposed to the pillaging of their historic photographic heritage by real specialists in the search for new collections.

It is also evident that photography has won a place for itself in Culture, generating a space of its own, but one which is widely shared by society as a whole. I have my doubts as to whether this has been achieved by the History of photography as such, and has not rather been the work of the mass media, which have created an international photographic iconography that is now recognized by any reasonably well-informed spectator. The fact is that photography as a cultural phenomenon is of interest to the general public, which is obviously not up to date with the debates and subtle nuances of the specialists; at the same time, there is an evident tendency to consider the photographic image from the perspective of art, and one does not need to be a visionary to foresee that the social expansion of the digital image will increase the *aura* of the photographic work in the near future.

Another aspect which has acted in favour of the historiography created by the Newhall school concerns the conditions of diffusion of its works. The History of photography is transmitted by means of books full of beautifully reproduced images, books that are aesthetically attractive and pleasing to look at and are now to be found on the shelves of many people who take an interest in culture. In this respect, Newhall's initial objective in 1937, the year in which he published the catalogue of the exhibition at the MOMA in New York that effectively launched this historiographic model, has been maintained over the years, coming to constitute a specialist branch of publishing which has innumerable readers all over the world.

For a present in transformation: the "Histories" of photography.

If at the present time a historian of photography were to attempt to construct her works on the basis of the 19th-century model of the Eder school and we then compared these with any of the existing histories of the photographic image which derive from to the tradition of the Newhall school, we would find ourselves faced with the paradox that these two visions are not in any way related to one another; they would be two parallel worlds, locked up in themselves and quite alien to one another. But if we were to practice that historiographic anachronism now, the other thing we would realize is that any historical study, however rigorous it may be, however well-founded, is still a work of creation on the basis of reality, a voluminous and chaotic body of material that in its totality is beyond the grasp of the human intellect.

But let us return to General History. If at the present time we can classify the sub-genre of historiography which deals with photography into two major consecutive schools, together with a series of specific smaller currents (Riego, 1994; Wells, 1997)[9], as far as General History is concerned, the most striking thing is that the great paradigms on which this had traditionally been grounded found themselves in crisis in the middle of the 20th century, and historians set out to explore two new directions, on the one hand incorporating into historical analysis instruments borrowed from other disciplines (economics, psychology, sociology, political theory, etc.), and on the other opening up the areas of investigation. While what was important for a classical historian was events, the deeds of the powerful or the history of nations, the new history that began to crystallize around 1970 set out to address new historical subjects coming to be considered just as important as the ones endorsed by the old-style historians. In this way, individual mentalities, private life, ethnic minorities, feminism, or the memory of those who had never made history, among others, began to be taken into account, accompanied by a search for methodological instruments with which to explain them and a break with the rigidity and the idolization in which historiographic discourse had previously been straitjacketed – a discourse that only concerned itself with the written documents produced by or for the established powers. New ways of explaining historical reality that called for new concepts as to what was to be under-

9 Liz Wells: *Photography. A Critical Introduction,* Ed. Routledge, 1997.

stood as a *document,* and in that process of renewal the photographic image emerged as an instrument of the first importance by virtue of its apparent immediacy and because, let us not forget, photography proved capable of responding to the multiple needs of contemporary society, not only the aesthetic, and this was an element which tied in very well with a new historiography that had greatly expanded its vision of the past.

And it was at this intersection that a new interest in photography was produced, to which schools such as that represented by the Newhall tradition are unable to give satisfactory responses because of the narrow conceptual framework they deploy. My own experience in this field can furnish a good number of examples of the way that leading experts in the new History, fascinated by the photographic document, have encountered insuperable difficulties in trying to assimilate into their work the categorizations of photographic history as these have been established, something which does not occur with other specializations, in which in spite of the inevitable difficulties of the translation between disciplines, there are points of conceptual exchange which this model evidently lacks. For this reason, one of the challenges facing those of us working in the more specialized areas of the History of photography is that of the integration of our work within the parameters of General History, of ensuring that our discourse is not particularist, and above all, that it should meet the conditions of rigour demanded by the universally accepted methodologies.

The fact is that the history of photography as such is not as homogeneous as it seems, and certain new lines of investigation have appeared in the last few years, thanks precisely to the emerging areas of interest to which the History is now turning its attention. A good example of these is the photography produced by women, which is giving rise to much interesting work, associated with the feminist cultural discourses, and a growing interest in cultural cross-fertilization over and above the tradition of anthropological photography. But the real leap forward has still to be made. This would be to understand the History of photography as such not in a monolithic sense, but as *ways of writing*, on different levels, which at times produce descriptive documents, at other times aesthetic products, and in the hands of other practitioners utilitarian truisms which are all too often of minimal value in terms of historical analysis. It is no longer possible to conceive of a single history based on famous photographers as canonic referents to be imitated or admired; we must point instead to the coexistence of diverse ways of understanding photographic culture, and subsume the results of these into the cultural tradition in which photography is nothing but one more instance among many of an interrelated complex. For example, it is impossible for us today to understand the 19th-century spectator as the receiver of the photographic images that were made and disseminated in her time, if we are not first capable of explaining the degree of graphic density which obtained at that time, as manifested by the various cultural forms in which the image played a predominant role, whether it be in the illustrated press, panoramas, dioramas, pictorial genres or set design in the theatre. And this is only one case, which can be transposed onto other moments in history in which photography is actively present. When we refer to the 20th century, when we speak of "new vision", we must not overlook, in seeking to comprehend that aesthetic phenomenon, the change in the conditions of political and social communication generated by a mass society: conditions to which photography is also capable of responding, whether it be in the press, or in the shaping of a new way of looking at the reality around us, as manifested in exhibitions and books. The very break itself that is being generated by the advent of the digital image is already beginning to reveal previously undetected tensions which can now be observed and incorporated into the analysis of historical events.

So, then, to sum up, we cannot overlook the fact that History fulfils functions over and above its discourse, the purpose of which is to arrive at an understanding of the past or to explain of the present by means of the tendencies produced by the past and which we have inherited in one form or another. History also fulfils functions in terms of cultural identity, situating phenomena and above all enabling us to understand the juncture at which we find ourselves, which is always one of the various possible options capable of taking place. The history of photography now has new challenges to face, at a point in time when the position of the spectator has also changed substantially (Crary 1993)[10], when culture is in the process of restructuring its functions and we are entering on a new reality that no longer has the linear and Cartesian character it had in the past. Within this scenario, a merely canonical interpretation of photographers and images does not seem to respond to our present-day needs.

Bernardo Riego, is a university lecturer and director of the Aula de Fotografía at the Universidad de Cantabria.

10 Jonathan Crary: *Techniques of The Observer*, Cambrigde, MIT Press, 1993.

GOOD-BYE, MR. NEWHALL
José Antonio Navarrete

"*Existe-t-il un objet de pensée que désignerait l'expression 'histoire de la photographie'?*" With this question Rosalind Krauss opens the section of her book *Le Photographique. Pour une Théorie des Ecarts* which brings together two of her essays on the history of 19th-century photography, originally published in English in the late 1970s and early 1980s, respectively. [1] However, before coming to these essays, the disciplined reader who has read the preface to the work, by Hubert Damish, and the general introduction, by Krauss herself, has had the opportunity to become aware that the author is not working on the much-travelled path of the history of photography as art; so, to quote Damish, whose words resonate with an echo of Walter Benjamin (1892-1940): "*la photographie ne se laisse pas réduire aux dimensions essentiellement 'stylistiques' que son celles de l'histoire de l'art*". [2]

1 Rosalind Krauss. *Le Photographique. Pour une Théorie des Ecarts*. Editions Macula, Paris, 1990. The two articles in question are "Sur les traces de Nacdar" and "Les espaces discursifs de la photographie", the first originally published under the title "Tracing Nadar" (October, #5, summer, 1978) and the second under the title of "Photography's Discursive Spaces" (*College Art Journal*, vol. 42, winter, 1982.)

2 Hubert Damish "À partir de la photographie". Preface to: Rosalind Krauss, op. cit., p. 10. As Benjamin remarks with reference to a calotype by Davis Octavius Hill (1802-1870) and Robert Adamson (1821-1848), taken around 1843. "(...) pictures, when they last, only last as a testimony of those who painted them. In the case of photography, on the other hand, something new and peculiar takes place: in the woman fish-monger of New Haven who looks down at the ground with a modesty that is so indolent, so seductive, there is something that cannot be reduced to the testimony of the art of the photographer Hill, something that cannot be silenced and that inexorably demands the name of the

Nonetheless, in the essays in question, Krauss' displacement of her object of study - nineteenth-century photography - from the space of art toward other discursive spaces, for all its undeniable critical fertility, takes as its platform of analysis an anachronistic understanding of the history of art- with a questionably subservient attitude to Benjamin and concessions to a long out-dated reductionism; on the one hand, this avoids addressing the complexity of meanings of the changes which took place in art under te specific conditions of modernity, and, on the other hand, it avoids incorporating into the context of the critique the contemporary demand for a rewriting of the history of art that oversteps those so frequently questioned limits that have prejudicially restricted it to a "history of styles". If we take this in conjunction with Krauss' obsession for excluding from her texts any historical information that would problematize her compulsive theses, it becomes inevitable that she leaves the issue of the historic relations between photography and art at the supposed point at which her chosen master had reached. The site of the debate, here, has its antecedents in the contradictory origins and the development of the history of photography as a specific discipline.

Constructing a discipline

The history of photography took shape as a discipline in the 1930s as a product of two epistemological models: the first, philosophical,

woman who lived there, who also in the effigy continues to be real and who can never be wholly reduced to art. (...)
Walter Benjamin, "Pequeña historia de la fotografía". In: Walter Benjamin. *Discursos interrumpidos*. Edit. Taurus, Madrid, 1973.

or, more precisely, sociological, subscribed to by Benjamin, a thinker of the Frankfurt School, at the beginning of the decade, within the framework of his reflections on the connections between social and technical evolution and the transformation of the status of the work of art; the second, anchored in the aesthetic paradigm, was forged in the intellectual and artistic circles of the North American *avant-guard* (primarily in New York), with the art historian Beaumont Newhall (1908-1993) being responsible for its initial comprehensive formulation, at the end of that decade. [3] As the reader will be aware, I am referring in the first case to the *Brief History of Photography*, 1931; in the second case, to the show presented in the Museum of Modern Art in New York (MOMA) under the title *Photography 1839-1937* and its respective catalogue, *Photography: A Short Critical History 1839-1937*, both from the latter year. [4]

3 This account can be found in a specialized dictionary. See: *Dictionnaire Mondial de la Photographie. Des origines à nos jours* (general editor: Jean-Phillippe Breuille). Larousse, 1994, pp. 300-301.

4 In "The Work of Art in the Age of its Mechanical Reproduction", an essay from 1936, Benjamin reused some of the aspects developed in the quoted next within a more complex theoretical framework. Beumont Newhall, at that time still officially the librarian of the New York Museum of Modern Art, curated the first retrospective exhibition of the history of photography in a museum of art, and published the catalogue in which he summed up his research on the subject. The exhibition was very well received in New York's artistic and critical circles, and toured the United States for two years. Other noteworthy early studies of the history of photography, such as the one by the German photographer Gisèle Freund, published in Paris in 1936 (*La Photographie en France aux dixneuvième siècle. Essai de sociologie et d'esthétique*) or the one by the North

The interpretation of the history of photography put forward by Newhall gradually became the dominant one. In his *History of Photography from 1839 to the Present Day* (George Eastman House/The Museum of Modern Art, New York), published in 1949, Newhall consolidated a model of historiography that was Eurocentric –concentrated on the axis composed of Germany, France, Great Britain and, with preponderant emphasis, the United States– and founded on the History of Art, which made the history of photography one of its specific branches. This model has served as the basis for the different versions of the "universal history" of photography produced by subsequent researchers up until quite recent times, and only occasionally expanded, as a rule, to include photographers of other nationalities within the course of this history [5]. However, when this work of

American scholar Robert Taft, published in New York in 1938 (*Photography and the American Scene. A Social History, 1839-1889*), are indications of the incipient organization of the history of photography as a particular discipline.

5 The privileged position of authority enjoyed by Newhall's *History of Photography* —revised and expanded in successive reprintings— is perhaps due not only to the erudition of its author or his other professional endowments, but also because Newhall was a historian of art with a firm committment to modern art and a modernist approach to the aesthetics of photography, and he created "its history" from the perspective of the latter, constructing the continuum that served to legitimate it. This ensured a long life for his focus, his authorial hierarchies and his conclusions. In addition, the art scene in the United States was from early on relatively favourable to the admission of photography into the highest levels of the institutional system of art, something which Newhall helped bring about through his pioneering work, and which at the same time allowed him to establish his reputation as a historian and curator of photography.

Newhall's consolidated its international reputation in the seventies, in the wake of the rise in the artistic status of photography in the field of Western art, alongside this there emerged other positions that were to give a radical and decisive turn to the history of photography as an object of study. These positions appeared to be linked, among other phenomena, to the growing interest within the French cultural milieu during the sixties and seventies in the sociology, semiology and ontology of photography, mainly under the aegis of structuralism and post-structuralism as nascent discourses of knowledge; to the resonance of Cultural Studies in Britain and the post-disciplinary character of this; to critical practice at the international level in relation to gender, race and ethnic issues, to the manifestations of this on the art scene and, in general, to the critique of representation in the cultural politics of what Hal Foster was to describe as "resistance postmodernism"; [6] and finally, to the emergence of the photographic patrimonies of the post-colonial world within the channels of international circulation of photography. The diffusion in the West of Benjamin's intellectual legacy during the late sixties and early seventies also served as a powerful stimulus for new historical approaches to photography.

[6] Hal Foster: "Introducción al posmodernismo" In: *La postmodernidad* (various authors, selection and Prologue by Hal Foster). Kairos, S.A., Barcelona, and Colofon, S.A., Mexico, 1988, p.11

De-centring

It is evident that in order for a radical transformation of the object of study of the history of photography to take place, there must first have been a shift in the way of engaging with photography itself. The centre of modernist interest in photography was based on so-called creative photography[7] —a broad concept that ended up by encompassing dissimilar and mutually contradictory artistic stances that, as a point in common, opted for an exploration of the "intrinsic" qualities of photography— and, on the basis of this as a privileged locus of thought, criteria of hierarchical distinction between the images produced by the camera were established; some of these images, always only a few, served to fuel the idea of photography as a radically new, radically modern expressive medium; others, the majority, did little more than satisfy the various forms of social demands. The recognition on the part of Modernist criticism and history that "good photographs" could also be produced by utilitarian photographic practices that did not set out to be artistic was yet another instance of the centring of their vision on the aesthetic, since in any case they were both constructed according to the individualizing principle inherent in art. When *Film und Foto*, an exhibition of long-lasting resonance, took place between May 18th and July 7th 1929 in Stuttgart, presenting the most recent tendencies in photog-

7 A term that was used primarily with reference to artistic photography, and therefore continued to be associated with the pictorialist photography which was severely criticized by the modernists.

8 Gustaf Stotz, "L'exhibition" In: *L'invention d'un art*. Centre Georges Pompidou, Paris, October 12, 1989 - January 1, 1990, pp. 110, catalogue..

raphy and cinema from the last ten years, Gustaf Stotz, the main conceptualizer of the event, explained:

> "In the first place, this exhibition has been put together with the aim of bringing together, where possible in their totality, the works of those figures who were the first to recognize the mechanism of photography as the medium of creation best suited to our age and, in consequence, the first to work with it. One of the tasks of this exhibition is, at the same time, to illustrate the new fields of action of photography, organizng these by groups and presenting a selection of images that are particularly characteristic of each one. Yet all of these works respect the same point of view: the apparatus on its own does not do anything. It is the human being who stands behind it and works with it who decides everything. I believe that in this way I have explained, in their essence, the concepts that inspired us to organize this exhibition in Stuttgart."[8]

When this centre was displaced, as a zone of thinking about photography began to be shifted away from the realm of photography as art object towards that of photography as text, as a representation to be deconstructed, the question of the contents and the social uses of the images came into the foreground. In any case, it is important to consider three factors associated with this epistemological change: first, the production of the whole range of photographic practices is incorporated into the study of society, without any kind of hierarchical structure, since photography is of interest above all as a document that communicates evident truths about a culture by means of a specific form of information: the visual; second, the recognition of the allegorical nature of photographic representation stimulates the study of both the historical relations between this and the ideological ordering of society and of its role in the diffusion of the corresponding legitimating discourses, including those of the scientific disciplines; finally, the enormous mass of photographic images, previously judged to be anodyne and irrelevant, take on a whole new splendour and become significant to the extent that they are a part of the challenges involved in the cultural strategy of rereading the narratives of modernism. All of this involved shakng up the very underpinnings of the foundations of a history of photography grounded in the authority of aesthetics; but, at the same time, it would be of the greatest value in understanding problems which arose at that time within the sphere of contemporary art itself. In 1981, in the paper that he delivered to the Second Latin American Colloquium on Photography, Mexico City, Néstor García Canclini, without abandoning the premisses of photography as a branch of art, proposed an expansion of the contents of the history of photography as a discipline that would thus include the very contents of art history as such. As Canclini remarked:

"The study of culture as a productive process involves considering all the steps of this process: production, circulation and reception. This being so we reject history books which conceive of art as a collection of objects. A photograph of the same nude woman acquires different meanings if it is published in an art history book, in a scientific review or in a pornographic magazine, if it is looked at by a man or a woman, from one social class or another. A good history of photography would be one that spoke not only about photographs and photographers, but also about the social uses of the images: a history of photographers, photographs, intermediaries and the public, of the relationships between these, the shifts from one social class to another, from one era to the next." 9

If the 1970s offered sporadic instances of ways of recounting the history of photography by freeing it from servitude to the exclusive interests of art, [10] the 1980s were still more productive in this respect. The object of the history of photography implanted in the field of knowledge of the discipline, in spite of its short existence, was being subjected to a constant problematization that was nonetheless unable to carry forward the corresponding systematic theorization. The existence of a multiplicity of practices within the field of photography, including the practice of art, the fruits of which were of tremendous importance for history, in conjunction with the mobility of many photographs –or of their ideological supports– from the terrain of certain practices to others, may well have discouraged any attempts at theorizing around the object of study of the history of a cultural product that was, by its very nature, promiscuous, omnirepresentational in its ambitions and documentary in character. [11] It would be necessary to investigate the point to which the indispensable theoretical premisses were drawn up –within the channels of the

9 Néstor Garcia Canclini, "Fotografía e ideología: sus lugares comunes". In: Hecho en Latinoamerica 2. Segundo Coloquio Latinoamericano de Fotografía. INBA, FONAPAS, CMF, A.C., Mexico, D.F., 1981, p.19

10 Susan Sontag's essays "on the meaning and history of photographs", published initially in *The New York Review of Books* and later brought together in her book *On Photography* (1977), were the most influential tests of their time for those who were no longer prepared to speak about the history of photography solely in terms of the epistemological model of art history.

11 Jose Antonio Navarrete, "Coleccionismo de fotografia: una tarea compleja". In: Jose Antonio Navarrete. *Ensayos disleales sobre fotografía*. CONAC-Fundaimagen, Mérida,1996, pp. 159-169.

enterprise of historiography as such, and with greater or lesser success– with a view to carrying out the particular tasks that this undertaking posited in each specific area.

Today, at the transition between two centuries, this situation seems quite normal. Perhaps, we ought first to demonstrate the possibility of speaking about the history of photography in different ways and of writing the history of society on the basis of photography, in order to gain a clearer view on the matter. What is more, the emergence of a new scenario within the field of photography, with the expansion of digital photography and the opening up of the virtual network as a space for the circulation of images, together with the increasing presence of art in the media –or more exactly, of artworks based on the media– on the contemporary art scene, have all helped to sideline, in the realm of the archeology of ideas, some of what seemed until quite recently to be enduring notions about ''the photographic'' that might have threatened the productivity of this theorization. It is only a few years since the Peruvian photographer and critic Fernando Castro offered the following prediction: ''(...) The new technology will transform researchers into archaeologists and photographers into archaic artisans, in so far as the image will embark on unimaginable courses.'' [12] So, then, in the light of these premises: how are we to satisfy the current need to rethink photography with the focus of history?

12 Fernando Castro, Commentary on Josune Dorronsoro's paper, ''Balance de la investigación histórica de la fotografía latinoamericana, desde fines de la década del setenta hasta la fecha'' In: *Memorias. Encuentro de Fotografía Latinoamericana,* Caracas, 1993. Consejo Nacional de la Cultura - Fundarte, Caracas, 1994, p.40.

A history of photography?

An aspiration towards the condition of art has been present in photography throughout the course of its history. At the same time, photography has brought about definitive modifications in the production, circulation and consumption of art and, as a consequence, in the very concept of art as such. A history of photography as the practice of art –and in its relations with art– seems to be of importance not only for the former, but also to a great extent for the latter. Of course, this would be a history of photography distinct from the one we have inherited. It would be a history motivated by reasoning about the way photography simultaneously acts both for and against art, more than in some contradictory movement of confrontation vs. renunciation with regard to it, in complicated and dissimilar forms of mutual collisions, contacts and exchanges.

It would be a history arising from the two finding themselves thrown together in a force field in which they constantly redesign their strategies of negotiation.

Rather than being based on stable notions of photography as a practice of art, or of art in general, it would be a history of the transformations that have been effected in these notions, whether in the space of encounter between the two or –in the case of the former– as a result of the flirtations and exchanges that take place between it and non-artistic practices.

If the crisis of modern Western culture, or, to be more precise, the crisis of its centrality, is a result of the emergence of the repressed or disenfranchised discourses contained within it, then this history must by the same token set out to recover the discursive fragments of the photographic practice of art which, due to their opposing, diverging from or –even more simply– situating themselves on the fringes of the constructive logic of the modernist history of photography, that history has silenced, neglected or at best compulsively articulated in pursuing its course. Even although this task has been successfully carried out in the advanced capitalist countries of the West –thanks to the public visibility that has been achieved by minorities and their discourses there– not all minority sectors have as yet benefitted to the same extent.

Within the framework of this same problem, one of the obligations which the history of photography faces today, as a practice of art, is that of abandoning its traditional Eurocentricism in order to adopt a multi-ethnic focus. Photography is a modern invention, bound to the international expansion of industrial capitalism, which was spread over the world by Europeans and North Americans and, no less significantly, one which corresponds to the convention of the central perspective that has been a part of the iconic tradition of the West since the Renaissance; but does this exclude the possibility of other aesthetic developments different from those which may have been configured within the Western continuum? Or more important still: are those developments that have evolved outside of the Eurocentric core, as well as in its sphere of influence, to be disqualified on the grounds of being mimetic? The Chinese curator and critic Hou Hanru recently observed in relation to this point:

> ''(...) in fact we can see a long history of non-Western photography, and this has a special significance, which is specifically what these non-Western cultures have appropriated and used as a tool of representation.

Thus, modernity has been written, rewritten, modified, and there are versions that have not only been those of the dominant Western cultures. (…) Thus, the production of images through electronic media, and this continuation of the "discovery" of photography, of course, includes not only the advances or the developments emerging from the global economic centres of the dominant cultures, but also includes all of these cultures which, while they did not originate photography, have substantially influenced the construction of the electronic image in the present age through their way of reacting. (…)" [13]

But, furthermore, a history of photography as a practice of art cannot base itself on an aesthetic axiology that undervalues the contexts of the artistic products, productswhich cannot be reduced to the exclusive criteria of language, form or style. As an object of study, art today can only engage with itself by taking into account the intense – and fecund – dialogue that it maintains with other social and cultural practices, including the constituted knowledges. As a prerequisite for the pursuit of less restricted possibilities for the comprehension of Its meanings and functions, the study of history asks to be configured as a place in which the knowledges and the methodologies developed by and borrowed from a whole range of disciplines come together. All of this has a bearing on a history of photography as a practice of art which would very readily go hand in hand with the indispensable rewriting of the history of art. [14]

13 Hou Hanru: José Antonio Navarrete and Guillermo Santamarina. Introduction to *Frontera*. 9th International Biennial Conference on Photography, Centro de la Imagen, Mexico City., 1999, pp. 7-8 (catalogue).

This expansion of the parameters of the object of study of the history of photography as a practice of art is a long way from exhausting –as we are aware– the possibilities of the history of photography. It is worth adding that some of the problems we have posited here intrinsically go beyond the artistic field. Photography as a practice of art is always a particular and specialized type of practice. Even though it communicates with other photographic practices, in contingent and sporadic movements of greater or lesser intensity, duration and meaning, its products have to be read and valued with reference to the history of it own praxis and to that of art in general. But there is no doubt that up until now the majority of photographs have been produced within the extra-artistic practices. In each of these practices voluminous bodies of work have been built up, more or less independently of one another, whose specific historicity provides a critical understanding of the processes of the practice in question, and of the particular field in which this practice is applied, whether it be journalism or fashion, anthropology or medicine. The object of study of the history of photography has multiplied and diversified with the appearance (as specific niches of study) of the histories of these photographic practices.

14 The art critic Gerardo Mosquera has frequently looked at the problems posited by the deconstruction of Art History as a discipline; among other texts, in the essay "Historia del Arte y culturas", published in *Revolucion y Cultura*, Ministerio de Cultura, Havana, volume IV, year 33, #6, November-December 1994, pp.27-29.

The determination to show everything that has, in spite of the impossibility of its being achieved, been associated with photography since its first beginnings, has also allowed it to establish itself –at different removes from the problematics of photographic practices– as the site of the historical investigation of a variety of social and cultural practices and, at the same time, of the forms of visibility of the discursive modes that circulate within the social framework, as we noted before; among the former, ranging from the practice of surveillance and punishment to that of work; among the latter, from the ideal of progress to that of identity. This has considerably expanded the realm of the historifiable in photography. At the present time, therefore, it seems advisable to speak not just about one but about several –perhaps many– histories of photography; not so much of a discipline as of a field of studies occupied by a multiplicity of positions. Instead of leading us to attempt to define the object of history of photography, the richness of this vast field asks us for a plural theorization in which, with regard to photography, history can shine forth as "rival of time, repository of actions, witness to the past, example and notice of the present, augur of what is to come": [15] is this an inappropriate goal?

José Antonio Navarrete, is a critic, editor of the magazine *ExtraCámara*.

15 Miguel de Cervantes, *El Ingenioso Hidalgo Don Quijote de la Mancha*. Edit. de Arte y Literatura, Havana, 1974, T. I, p. 75.

REFLECTIONS FOR A
NEW HISTORY OF PHOTOGRAPHY
Carmelo Vega

As a preliminary step in attempting to define what should be the conceptual and methodological parameters on which to found a history of photography, it is necessary to reflect briefly on the ways of writing the history of the medium, or, in other words, on the prevailing models and on the strategies of analysis of the photographic image as a historical phenomenon.

This issue, which is currently arousing an extraordinary level of interest, on the Spanish scene at least, is not exempt from certain paradoxes; first of all, because many of those models (for example, Beaumont Newhall's) were established in their day as an emergency formula for the purpose of organizing a discipline that until then had been without shape or structure. Those proposals that were posited as an immediate initial solution to a specific problem nonetheless ended up as narrow, orthodox patterns, imitated by subsequent generations of researchers working on photography.

A second paradox, more evident in the case of Spain, is the existence of a model of the history of photography without a model (almost always applied at a local or regional level), on top of which a general historical framework is superimposed with the aim of serving as a point of reference. The methodological fragility of many of these studies stems not so much from adopting this reductionist and geographically-limited schema —almost always unconnected to any overall vision— as from shortcomings in the education of the historian. When all is said and done, who produces or has produced the history of photography? The absence of a specialized discipline in the Spanish university environment has meant that the various contributions to the field of the history of photography have come from uninformed perspectives lacking, in certain cases, the appropriate methodological supports. The work of the historian of photography who, at the present time, considers her or his activity as a task of renewal, needs to start from an in-depth critique of the values sanctioned as the necessary parameters of a history of photography. In this respect, it seems to be relevant to resolve a couple of questions, such as: on what premisses should we regenerate the history of photography? Or, from what standpoint do we validate our position as historians?

The first measure to be taken in this process of decanting a new history of photography would consist in defining with some exactitude the actual object to be included under the generic label of photography, at the same time clarifying the point of view from which we approach this object. In my opinion, it would be not so much a matter of questioning the possibility of photography as a historicizable subject as such, as of the fact of defining what it is about photography that we are interested in historicizing: this is what Régis Durand calls the "possible histories" of photography (the history of the appearance, of the fixing or the reproduction of the photographic image, the history of photography as a technique –procedures, apparatus, optics, formats– or the history of the uses of photography). Even while allowing the theses that endorse the difficulty of giving historical shape to the field of the photographic, we should not forget that photography, by virtue of its very complexity, encompasses a set of phenomena –on the technical as well as on the theoretical and aesthetic level– that in all probability cannot be separated from one another without creating fissures that would alter their meaning. The task of the historian is not only to draw up mere inventories of events and anecdotes or to put together catalogues of the work of individual photographers, nor is it to organize their biographies, nor to compile eloquent quotations, nor to turn history into an evolutionary exposition of stylistic descriptions of photographic images. The exercise of history would consist in giving shape to a set of independent variables that, properly fitted together and interpreted, would offer us the key to understanding the specific mentality and the particular forms of expression of a man in his time.

In this respect, and as an art historian, it seems to me that exclusive or unidirectional models only serve to hinder an overall vision of the phenomenon of photography. As a discipline linked to the analysis of images and as one with a longer and earlier tradition, Art History offers prior methodological experiences and stances which have subsequently been repeated by scholars of photography: ranging from a history conceived as a hagiography of the great names to a history that welcomes all classes of "minor" productions (according to the obsolete terminology still used by some art historians), such as anonymous or amateur photographs; from a history of the technical and material factors to a history of photographic forms; from a history of commitment and ideologies to a history of perception; from an iconography of photographic motifs to a history of photography from the perspective of the aesthetics of reception.

Obviously, this is not to say that historians of photography are obliged to resort to each one of these models of analysis in order to articulate their studies. All of these methodological systems are only possible facets that guarantee a explanation of the whole and serve to enrich an integral reading of photography.

The incorporation of the history of photographic images into the domain of the history of art –understood as the history of images– has frequently been rejected by those who defend photography as an autonomous and differentiated discipline. While this is not the place to ponder this problem in depth, it is indeed worth clarifying a few points. It is true that art historians, up until a few years ago, had felt no need to become familiar with and explore the fundamental values of photography; it functioned only as an illustration of the work of art, as a mere reproduction and not as an image derived from a distinct creative process and as such susceptible to analysis on the part of Art History.

From the field of photography, too, there was frequently a reluctance to accept openly this relationship. Thus, for example, it is necessary to understand the conceptual problems which still existed in the 1950s that Alsina Munné (*Historia de la Fotografía*. Barcelona, 1954) had to face in attempting to define the "notion of photography as art". To speak of art in reference to photography was, for him, synonymous with being "polemical". Could photography, he wondered, place itself, "even if only secondarily", alongside painting, sculpture and poetry? In his opinion, there was a middle ground for photography: a "new zone" located between Fine Art –"absolute arts"– and the applied arts.

In spite of this, the leading role which photography has acquired in the last few decades and its involvement in contemporary artistic experiences have caused the history of art to start to look again at photography from a new perspective: photography is now considered not only as an image that has influenced movements and tendencies in art during the last two centuries (the contaminating character of photography, according to some), but also as embodying and summing up in itself the conflictive nature of contemporary art as such. In this sense, and as we have pointed out already on other occasions, photography is a symptom of the transformations which, from the middle of the 19th century, began to take place in the very concept of art.

Strange as it may seem, it is probable that at the present time the history of art may need photography more than photography needs the history of art. In spite of this, when we speak of the history of art as a framework (not the sole framework, but merely a possible framework) for the study of photography as a historical phenomenon, we do so in the conviction that photography, like other iconic forms of expression and creation, is a response in images to the problems and expectations of a particular era; photography –like painting, poetry, cinema or music– is, first and foremost, a declaration of the sensibility of a time. Consequently, if photography is part of the sum of human creative expression, It also shares with other forms of creation the same principles and postulates, the same causes and effects. Thus, photography would be the manner in which uti lizing its own resources and procedures– human beings translates his vision of the world, or in other words, the way in which the world is expressed in photographic terms.

How, then, are we to explain photography as an isolated and non-referential phenomenon, as an autonomous discipline which is self-sufficient and justifiable in its own terms. According to this version, photography and its history could only be explained in any coherent way by the photographer in person (a fragile means of ensuring an absolute autonomy: history makes it the subject of its own history). In opposition to the purist isolation of photography, I would regard

an interconnected relationship with other simultaneous expressions
of the creation of images as much more productive, without this implying a renunciation of everything that makes photography distinctively
what it is. In short, I believe it is possible to have an Art History which
is capable of taking on the study of photography without questioning
its specificity, valuing in a positive sense –as an attribute and not a
defect– what makes it different from other images is, and adapting
the conceptual, formal and terminological contributions specific to
photography to the analysis of contemporary art.

Perhaps one of the most interesting contributions made by photography to the debate on artistic creation revolves around the concept
of the artist. We are referring here not only to the dialectic derived
from the relation established between the creator and the technological mechanism which significantly modifies the role traditionally
assigned to the artist. Rather, we are interested in this problem to the
extent to which it also has a bearing on certain methodological positions when it comes to engaging with a history of photography. Rosalind Krauss, for example, questions the application of concepts such
as artist and artwork in the sphere of photography, citing a number
of paradigm cases which invite us to reflect on the dilemma of putting
forward a history of photography from the perspective of a history
of photographers or a history of images.

With reference to the artist, Krauss mentions the case of certain individuals in the 19th century who were only photographers for a short
part of their lives –"can you imagine someone being an artist for
only one year?"– and gave it up almost immediately, yet in spite of
this they are now depicted as key figures in any history of photogra-

phy. In this context, it would be useful to reconsider the way in which the historian organizes the recovering of a photographer's work, in order to avoid certain excesses and errors of judgement; it is quite often the case, for example, that photographers whose work is strictly second-rate or of only minor importance are rediscovered and presented (for reasons of ignorance, of a lack of a overall vision, or of vested interest) as if they were creators of unquestionable value, or that, in the attempt to adapt their work to certain dominant discourses, the original intention of the photographer is distorted.

We all know that the photographer's archive is a space of accumulation, and, in most cases, of disorder: there we find photographic materials of all sorts, in a variety of formats and supports, all of them potentially cataloguable objects, but objects that need to be filtered by the specialist if they are not to produce major distortions in the reading of the photographer's work (what is to be done, for example, with the same negative copied by the author himself using different procedures or on different occasions in the course of his life; what is to be done with photographs thrown away or rejected by the photographer; or, as Krauss points out, how are we to distinguish and evaluate the work done by the studio assistants and not by the photographer himself, and how are we to evaluate the "unfinished" works?). Furthermore, in every historical examination of the body of photographic material there is an additional quantitative problem that tends to confuse the researcher: it is common for the photographer's archive to be made up of thousands (or tens of thousands) of photographs, many of them realized with a meaning and for a purpose different from those that the contemporary observer looks for and interprets. A rigorous practice of the history of photography would thus entail an adapting of the historian's vision to the original vision of the photographer, something that is only partially possible, given that a history lacking in a certain critical spirit ends up as a mere chronicle devoid of content. This is, indeed, a danger –a methodological virus– that is always associated with the photographic image, and which at times causes the history of photography to lose its way and become an illustrated history of images of the past: in order to create a true history of photography, it is necessary to look at photographs without nostalgia.

From a different point of view, even though it may appear to contradict the one outlined above, we have to admit that photography as a historical phenomenon is subject to a profound ignorance, not only on the part of the general public, but also on the part of the specialists. In effect, what do we really know about the history of photography? It is not only the way in which we experience photography (almost always through reproductions), but the fact that a great number of the images which almost all of us associate with the history of the medium come from the context of particular museums or collections, and are thus affected by the dynamic of the mechanisms that habitually serve to mythologize certain photographers or those of their works in the possession of a given museum or collection: the photograph thus becomes a piece, an object which the institution is interested in making more widely known, and this constant dissemination ends up converting it into a "masterpiece", a classic of photography. In line with the model established by writers such as Gernsheim or Newhall (themselves curators, the former of the Gernsheim Collection at the University of Texas in Austin, and the latter of both the photography department of the Museum of Modern Art in New York and the George Eastman House collection), recent publishing ventures put forward an organization of the history of photography on the basis of the material available in the holdings of certain museums and collections; thus, for example, two recent books for a general readership from the publishing house Taschen (*20th Century Photography* and *Photography from 1839 to Today*) put together their histories of photography from the material in the archives of the Ludwig Museum in Cologne and those of the George Eastman House in Rochester.

Another significant element of distortion in certain histories of photography, especially those by French and English-speaking writers, is the evidently national character of their content, in giving a specially significant role, both in the first moments of the emergence of photography and in the subsequent course of events, to photographers from their own country. This approach, reductionist yet again, imposes itself as a model for other places: the other histories of photography –those of the countries that took up the inventions and proposals of the French and British– seem to make sense only in relation to the work produced in or from those countries. The formula is copied, or the guidelines for an explanation of the history of photography are followed; what is lacking is the critical spirit, the revolt against the imposed model, the revision of the criteria of analysis; in short, what is lacking is a new history of photography.

Carmelo Vega, is a professor at the Universidad de La Laguna and historian.

THE HISTORY OF PHOTOGRAPHY, A HISTORY OF PHOTOGRAPHIES

Daniel Girardin

There has never been, and maybe there will never be, such a thing as an all-round history of photography. Nor is there a single "history of art" or an all-inclusive "history of architecture". What there are, however, are the multiple histories of an extraordinary medium, as far as photographic creation is concerned, and a field that holds enormous potential in terms of both research and analysis.

Approximately twenty histories were written in the 20th Century after Josef Maria Eder[1] wrote his "History of Photography" in 1905. In their writings, the authors were mainly concerned with technology or chronology and in doing so revealed how limiting such an approach can be. Examples of this are Beaumont Newhall[2] (1937), Raymond Lecuyer[3] (1945), Helmut and Alison Gernsheim[4] (1955) and Naomi Rosenblum[5] (1984).

In the most recent publication to date (1994), Michel Frizot[6], as head of a team of experts, chose to focus on the photographs themselves and to highlight the creative domain into which they fall rather than their chronological order. By uniting historical research and

1 Josef Maria Eder, Geschichte der Photographie, New York : Dover, 1978 (1st edition Berlin, 1905).

2 Beaumont Newhall: *The History of Photography from 1839 to the Present*, London: Seker and Warburg, 1982 (1949).

3 Raymond Lécuyer: *Histoire de la photographie*, Paris: Baschet, 1945.

4 Helmut Gernsheim / Alison Gernsheim: *The History of Photography*, London: Oxford University Press, 1955.

5 Naomi Rosenblum: *Une histoire mondiale de la photographie*, Paris: Flammarion, 1998 (1989).

photographic theory, this work stands in a field of its own, since the latter, unfortunately, has often had little to do with existent historical research, itself either monographic, aesthetic or chronological. The question of the gap between the various photographic theories and the different "histories of photography" is what is really at the heart of the matter. This can partially be explained by the fact that, in general, most historical texts in the past were written by collectors or curators who had little if any contact with the universities. Consequently, the critical wherewithal and histiographic insight were lacking. Most of these histories evolved in parallel to and were given prominence by the exhibition of their various collections. The stakes were more direct but they also conditioned an approach that avoided the question of theory in favour of aesthetic appreciation, in which personal interpretation became preponderant.

The quality of the "New History of Photography", as initiated by Frizot, is proof that the era of the singular, personal and encyclopaedic understanding of photography is a thing of the past, giving way to a collective approach based on the idea of a genuine "photographic culture". Another merit of this work is that it does not adhere to the methods that apply to the history of art and in doing so frees itself from the models that are not inherent to photography itself.

Photography, as a discipline in its own right, is relatively new and has only emerged in European universities over the past ten years or so. In addition to this, it covers a vast field since the photograph is

6 Michel Frizot (under the supervision of): *Nouvelle histoire de la photographie,* Paris: Bordas/ Adam Biro, 1994.

not only associated with the series and the commonplace, it is also connected to every other discipline within our culture, whether it be artistic, social, historic or scientific.

It must also be said that this call for new methods of analysing the image comes at time when the history of art is undergoing a crisis, in so much as it is unable to get to grips with the photograph, the video or the digital age. In addition, there is a need for a new approach that addresses the sociology of the family photograph, the use of photography in the industrial context or the riveting subject of anonymous photography.

Any project on "The History of Photography" must face two major questions: the extent of the range of activities that photography covers and the analytical methods that are specific to it. Photography is an art, sometimes it is even more and often it goes well beyond the question of art. It is a means of mass communication but it is also a means of aesthetic and subjective expression that results from a particular way of looking.

Photography is the art of looking. However, what the photograph signifies is beyond the control of its creator and its link with the real world makes it very difficult to grasp the ambiguities and paradoxes that hide behind it. Since the beginnings of photography, there have been tremendous subversive forces at work, and the proofs against photographic reality have mounted up, but they have not yet been able to overturn preconceived ideas or prejudice.

The photograph is both an object (a print on paper) and a subject (the content). The latter can appear on various supports (on paper or postcards, in books, as a digital image etc.) and can be sold in any form.

But what gives the photograph its value today, in the flourishing art market, is the quality, as much as the scarcity, of the print.

Over the past fifty years, certain ideas have given rise to considerable controversy. One example, which stemmed from the tradition of engraving, is that of "*vintage*". The result has been positive in so much as it has laid bare the different facets of photography's status; in the aesthetic and artistic spheres first of all, but also in that of the art market and the museum. For instance, the concept of "*vintage*" has given the published photograph a whole new meaning and allowed the photographer to claim the right to authorship, something that had previously been difficult to defend or even take before a court of law.

The theoretical history of photography today comprises thousands of monographs, studies, analyses, comparisons and research papers based on analytical methods that are specific to other disciplines, particularly to the history of art, semiology, anthropology, psychoanalysis, philosophy (the phenomenology of perception in particular), the history of science or the history of culture.

It also comprises the innumerable texts that have been published since the official invention of photography, including the writings that Nicéphore Niépce wrote himself and that we are discovering today thanks to modern publications.

A lesser-known part of this history was produced by certain photographers who, in some cases, wrote perfect photographic "manifesto*s*". This was true, for example, of the periods known as "pictorialism" and "straight photography" and of various photographic avant-garde movements in the 1920's, it is also true of Robert Frank in the 50's and more recently of certain post modern artists.

The history of important exhibitions over the past century and the study of the strategies adopted by museums, galleries and specialised institutions must also be envisaged. An exhibition such as *The Family of Man* by Edward Steichen followed by the publications and exhibitions by John Szarkowski who, as curator of the Museum of Modern Art in New York, took a critical stance with regard to the concepts of his predecessor, contributed greatly to the debates on photography. There are many traditional approaches which trace the advance of photographic technology out of an underlying conviction that the aesthetic potential of this discipline is determined by techniques. Certain publications are more concerned with the chronological order of events and tend to follow the various schools and photographic practices: documentary photography, for instance, pictorialism, ''straight'' photography, the avant-garde, fashion, the free-lance, photojournalism and more recently, the photograph that is produced specifically for the museum.

Each analysis is oriented by different considerations, be they social, historical, aesthetic, artistic, political, ideological or merely factual. There is no single interpretation of photography, only complementary logics. What is important is that in each instance, the tools used for analysis should be pertinent to this discipline and take into account the historical, intellectual and cultural environments in which the photographs were created as well as the context of their dissemination.

We know, for instance, that the aesthetic aspect of a photograph is accentuated over time and that a photograph is interpreted according to the experience, fantasies and nostalgia of the spectator. That a photograph is a symbolic appropriation of the world and of those that live in it, and that it is able to "*aestheticise*" some of the most atrocious acts of humanity. That the photograph is the result of coded cultural models, that it is the vector of powerful ideologies and that it is a western means of expression that is all too often *ethnocentric*. That furthermore, it is more of a means to knowledge than a genuine historical or ethnographic record and that its interpretation is difficult due to the *logocentric* nature of our culture. The title can radically change the meaning of a photograph. The surrealists understood the creative potential of the various associations that arise from the juxtaposition of the photograph and language.

The photographer is an integral part of the process, both by his presence and his personality. Equally, he has always straddled two industries: the manufacturing of cameras, negatives and paper on the one hand, and the circulation of images on the other, something that can only be partially controlled and even then, for no more than a certain length of time.

Art historians are perhaps the most qualified to analyse the photograph because they have the formal and methodological means to do so at their disposal. However, art historians have tended to overlook photography, even though it has revolutionised their discipline. Having fallen into the trap that consists of regarding photography as the impoverished result of mechanical reproduction and giving unilateral credence to its analogical character, art historians have often been complacent and held photography in contempt. Photography has long been considered at worst as a technique and at best as a minor art.

19th Century academic prejudice hindered considerably the possibility of analysing photography, within the traditional discipline of the history of art, in a way that was both original and specific to photography itself. Caught between the crisis in painting and the birth of the cinema, photography was not to have its own distinctive philosophy until the 20th Century.

Furthermore, some of the best texts on photography have been written by authors, such as Roland Barthes, [7] who were critical of it, or who, like Walter Benjamin, [8] knew little about it. Such writers were able to have a completely fresh approach and to angle their critical theory in a way that gave an in-depth understanding to one aspect of photography in particular.

Art historians could contribute a great deal in helping to understand the status of photography and its place in the history of image production in the west. The history of photography should be seen as part of a movement that stretches from the tradition of the Holy Shroud and other such "Sindons" to the plates in the 18th Century *Encyclopédie* and includes the altercations between *iconodules* and *iconoclasts* as well as the Renaissance, and the ideologi-

7 Roland Barthes: *La chambre claire. Note sur la photographie,* Paris: Gallimard, 1980.

8 Walter Benjamin: "Petite histoire de la photographie", in: *Poésie et Révolution,* Paris: Denoël, 1971 (1931); Walter Benjamin: "L'ouvre de l'art à l'ère de sa reproductibilité technique", in: *Poésie et Révolution,* Paris: Denoël, 1971 (1936); Walter Benjamin: *Sur l'art et la photographie,* Paris: Carré, 1997.

cal ideals of beauty and truth that photography has, in some cases, brought to the fore.

There have been too few studies into the historical, scientific, cultural or economic conditions that presided over the invention of photography. Why and how did the very idea of photography come about? Since all the necessary technical and scientific conditions were in place almost a century before Niepce produced his first positive results, why did it take so long? Research into this field would be invaluable in improving the general understanding of photography, its development and usages. [9]

Complete collections of photographs, from the 19th Century in particular, went straight from their archive boxes into museum collections, shedding the ancillary status of "*iconographic documents*" for the coveted status of museum piece. In the same way, certain prints which only thirty years ago were of little worth, are sold for thousands today.

It is clear that this trend is positive but the discourse it engenders is not always coherent or understood outwith specialised circles.

The long list of difficulties that such a large-scale project must face, the broad outlines of which have been given here, shows just how ambiguous a "*history of photography*" can be: a subject that arouses passionate interest on the one hand but presents philosophical and conceptual difficulties on the other. Any future project that takes a pluralist and novel approach will have to take all these difficulties

9 See for instance, Nicéphore Niépce: *Une nouvelle image*, Chalon sur Saône: Société des Amis du Musée Nicéphore Niépce, 1999.

into account. In the digital age, it will perhaps be easier to conceive of the evolution of photography in a more open and synthetic manner, in so far as the latter, in the not too distant future, will have become a very classic means of expression.

But the outcome will never be totally convincing as long as the main point has not been established, namely, the recognition of the preponderant role of photography in our culture.

Daniel Girardin, Curator of the Musée de l'Elysée in Laussanne.

REFLECTIONS ON THE HISTORY OF PHOTOGRAPHY*
Boris Kossoy

I would guess that all of us who work in the history of photography find ourselves grappling in the early stages of our researches with the weight of the classical models of the history of photography; and I also believe that some of us are led, at a given moment in time, to question the validity of such models from the specifically historical point of view, as well as from a broader cultural perspective. From the very first I was struck by the episodic nature of the histories of photography, by their markedly positivist cast and their lack of any kind of conceptual orientation.

Right from the outset I realized that it was truly exceptional to find a multidisciplinary approach to, and in, the histories of photography. It is evident that this kind of 'take' would first of all require an understanding of this historical genre within a wider cultural perspective. And in terms of ideology, it is obvious that this was never the aim of the dominant models (given that it would entail the need for a knowledge and a critical evaluation of the historical facts in all their social, economic, cultural and ideological ramifications), dangerous territory for those who sought only to enumerate events without knowing anything of the causes that gave rise to them. The dominant models constitute authentic archaeologies of dispersed documents that are devoid of the causal connections that drive the movement of history.

In seeking to break down these models, I have observed that I was confronting a written history fashioned in a spirit that seems to be closer to botany than to the social sciences. I have noticed that certain facts (always the same ones) tended to be classified technically and aesthetically in specific categories and in closed compartments. This amounted to a 'methodology of classification' of facts and photos having no connection with the earth, with blood, suffering, emotion; in other words, with something that had been generated in a given space, at a particular moment in time. The treatment is more or less the same, irrespective of the subject matter. Even in the case of scenes of battle, the images were always treated as something 'innocent', as no more than images captured on paper without any *interior reality*, divorced from the historical fact, from the emotion and the ideology of their creators. Pure illustrative images. What was normally done –and is still done today– was to borrow certain aesthetic concepts from the history of art and apply these to photography.

The classical models of the history of photography such as those of Gernsheim and Newhall, among others, were first developed in the course of the 40s and 50s and subsequently brought up to date; panoramic works (which concentrated on the United States and the countries of Europe that have always been seen as 'civilizing frameworks'). 'World' histories of photography that are, however, confined within certain geographical limits drawn on the basis of ideology. 'World' histories of photography in which Africa, Asia and Latin America, for example, are excluded by the absolute lack of any historical, aesthetic or cultural interest in them. Continents that have been left on the fringes of history, and countries in which photography went entirely unnoticed. It had no history.

These works became beacons of knowledge, they came to constitute references because there were no others. In them, what has always been emphasized is the technical procedures and the aesthetic focus

in isolation from, among other things, their context; models characterized by vast accumulations of data and no critical analysis. In
any case, those (institutionalized) premisses ended up constituting
a pattern of historical narrative that has been followed for a considerable period of time now and has had innumerable adherents
all over the world.

So it is that Newhall, Gernsheim and other writers have all suffered from the same errors, in their failure to link the history of photography to the socio-historical context. What we do have are photographic facts decontextualized from their social reality. The result
is that the images which illustrate their books are *divorced from the
conditions of production that gave rise to them*. Nowadays, it is no
longer possible to analyse or interpret an image solely on the basis
of its 'aesthetic values' in isolation from the ideology of its creator
(and that of the people who commissioned it), from the history of
the actual subject treated (independently of the representation) and
from the use that has been made of this same representation. All of
this is the result of the complete absence of conceptual grounding in
the issues specific to the problem of photographic sources understood
as *historical sources*. It also has to do with the ideology that determines how history is written. I would like to pause here to consider
a few examples.

For certain writers, what has taken place —and continues to take
place— in the Third World is 'exotic' because it is different and evidently of no interest in terms of the ethnocentric patterns implicit in
their view of the world. Such subject matter might be of interest, at
the most, in the way it *exemplifies* the opposites, that is to say the

tropical, the underdeveloped, the backward, the typical, the Latin, the inferior, etc. Exemplifications that operate on two levels, in that they end up revealing the inherent prejudices, the mental image their user has of the *other*. Perhaps the best example of one of these 'compartmentalised' subjects is so-called ethnographic photography, where at the back of the virtual 'thematic interest' there lies prejudice. That mentality was incorporated into the thinking of the producers of culture in its various forms.

In *Image and Memory* I set out to demonstrate the extent to which photographic representation would have served to reinforce the ethnocentrist posture of the white European male when he addresses the realities of Latin America in a globalizing fashion. The photographic record, with all the load of ambiguities that characterize it, can be seen as perverse (or efficient?), given that in general it lends itself to legitimating the mental images that the spectator has formed on certain subjects. This means that the photographic image 'confirms' and therefore transforms into material 'truth' all that is immaterial and ideological in mental images. In other words, it transforms fiction into reality, fantasy into truth and preconceived ideas into *concrete facts, once these have been confirmed by means of the photographic document*: in this way, the imaginary takes on flesh.

That mentality, that approach to those ethnographic subjects in terms of 'the European gaze' and the forms in which these were represented/documented reinforced a certain concept of Latin America. The photographic representations of such subjects from the past imply, ambiguously, in their exterior/interior aspect the concept (or prejudice?) in line with the intentions for which they were produced and used. That same mentality was transplanted to the history of photography, both in the earliest works and in recent studies.

The Latin-American photographic experience, with respect to both the craft of photography and the image of the persons or things portrayed, was in reality a *European experience*. Meanwhile, to offset this there was an *exotic experience* of Latin America in Europe in the 19th century, as a consequence of the ideological use of the so-called photographic testimony that made concrete the preconceived mental images of those tropical realities.

If the historians of photography *were aware* that certain ethnographic images are products of ethnocentric and racist ideologies –as these were produced and transmitted in the past when (pseudo) scientific racial theories were in vogue, and as they were (and continue to be) reproduced in the history books– they would certainly now be opening up a space for the study of minorities and disadvantaged groups, broadening the at times extremely narrow limits of that history.

The specific research work has multiplied in many different places, bringing to light facts and images that are of unquestionable importance in enabling specialists in the area to arrive at a wider vision and a wider understanding of the history of photography, which is thus no longer a sphere of knowledge exclusively confined to the industrialized nations. Thanks to the work that has been carried out, we now have a fair idea of who the pioneering photographers in these countries were, where they came from, what influences they exercised, and how the expansion of photography took place, among other matters. The state of near total –or at least seriously distorting– ignorance that prevailed until quite recently in relation to the origins and the evolution of photography in geographical spaces outside of the United States and certain European countries is beginning to change. At the same time, a fundamental part has also been played by the new approaches, whose expansion has made a decisive contribution in helping specialists working in the area to perceive the different treatments that the old subjects seem to deserve.

What is more, there is no longer any need for anyone with an interest in this area of knowledge who lives in a major city to be ignorant of the histories of other regions of the planet. However, there is still a certain xenophobic resistance, for example, on the part of certain writers to the ground-breaking work with photosensitive materials carried out by Hercules Florence in 1833 in the interior of the State of São Paulo (Brazil), which culminated in their independent discovery in the Americas. The lack of awareness of Florence's discovery on the part of the general public seems to me to be disturbing precisely to the extent that it is here, in this realm of disinformation, that historical truth is reduced to the status of anecdote, legend or fiction. And this is also the void space in which those who reject the progress of knowledge hold sway, the territory of the opportunists, specialists in the omission and deformation of the historical facts.

The discomfort felt by some at this discovery is itself indicative of the ethnocentrist attitude and its inability to come to terms with the idea that certain achievements of the human spirit can (and do) take place *beyond the traditional geographical limits of 'civilization'*, meaning, in effect, the major centres of production and dissemination of culture in its multiple manifestations. In this regard, the work carried out Hercules Florence, in a setting far removed from the *ideal spaces,* exemplify this very well, and clearly constitute a new phenomenon that contributes to and enriches the history of photography and of culture. In one way or another, several of the canonical authorities have incorporated this new phenomenon, even if only timidly.

In any case, the task of the historian is to contribute to the construction of knowledge, and the question of whether that knowledge is rapidly adopted and assimilated or not is a cultural and ideological issue that goes beyond the historian's function.

The history of photography is very often confused with the history of photographic technique, or with the history of the photographers themselves, of their images, etc., when in fact it embraces these and other histories within its field of study. The history of photography is also the history of its applications, of its uses; however, the ideology of those applications has to be understood in depth. There is a need for both a history of photographers and a history of images. The two are the *body and soul* of the history of photography: indivisible by definition.

In the photographic image we find, inseparably incorporated, components of a *material order* that are the indispensable resources –technical, optical, chemical or electronic– for the materialization of photography and components of an *immaterial order*, which are mental and cultural. The latter superimpose themselves hierarchically on the first, and articulate with them in the mind and in the actions of the photographer in the course of a complex *process of creation*. The question, as we find it represented in the photographic image, is the product of a series of choices; it is the outcome of a number of options of different kinds, thought out and selected by the photographer; choices that follow more or less concomitantly and interact with one another, determining the nature of the representation.

In using the images of the past as a primordial source, the historian is necessarily involved in the decoding of the artefact and its visible, external face, its *exterior reality*, and in the deciphering of its hidden, internal face, its *interior reality*. However, an interpreter who does not have an in-depth knowledge of the historical period portrayed will never grasp what the images of the past have to show, wandering eternally over their iconographic surface talking about 'aesthetic values'.

The contextualization of photographers and images in their specific historical moment is of fundamental importance. The photographic image can basically emphasize a single subject, but it also provides the basis for innumerable investigations; opening up a whole series questions of a political, social, economic and religious nature. Aesthetics and ideology are fluid components of the photographic representation, hence the importance of knowing what lies behind the image. *We cannot understand the history of photography in isolation from the history of culture.*

The study of the photographic sources always calls for inter- and multidisciplinary approaches, which means that the history of photography itself cannot escape this condition. The genesis and the history of photographic documents, and of the fragments of the visible world of the past that those same documents preserve in frozen form, require for their proper understanding a wide range of information from many different areas of knowledge. Whatever the contents of the images, we should always regard them as historical sources with a multidisciplinary scope. Sources of information that are decisive for their respective uses in the different fields of historical research, in addition, of course, to the history of photography itself. The photographic images do not end in themselves; on the contrary, they are only points of departure, the clues that let us attempt to unveil the past. They provide us with a selective fragment of the appearance of things, of people, of events, as these were aesthetically/ideologically frozen in a given moment of their existence/occurrence. For this reason, the subject, once it has been represented in the image, is *a new datum*: dramatized, deformed, aesthetically revalued, idealized, or to put it another way, *ideologized*. It is clear that we are dealing with a new reality, that of the photographic image, which I some time ago described as a *second reality*.

In common with the various other sources of historical information, photographs cannot immediately be accepted as faithful mirrors of the facts. And photographs, like those other documents, also entail a wealth of ambiguities, as the bearers of meanings that are not explicit and of deliberate, calculated omissions, waiting to be competently deciphered. Their potential to inform can be achieved only in so far as these fragments are contextualized in the mesh of history, in the multiple ramifications (social, political, economic, religious, artistic, cultural) that circumscribed in time and space the act of their taking. If this were not so, those images would be left enclosed in their silence: disconnected fragments of memory, mere 'artistic' illustrations of the past.

So complex is the history of this medium of communication and expression that, in embracing a extensive repertoire of questions of different natures, it will always tend to resort to the aid of a whole range of disciplines, which is positive, given that it will constantly renew its objects of study and the way it interprets these. Nor can other areas of research that utilize images of the past do without the specific bodies of knowledge accumulated by means of the histori-cal studies of photography themselves. It is a matter, then, of re-eval-uating our appreciation of the photographic sources, both in the realm of the history of photography and with regard to the use made of that history in other areas of historical research. At the same time, the his-tory of photography can no longer be seen as merely a succession of episodic facts and accounts of events (illustrated with images); instead, we should be seeking –with due regard for the specificities of this his-torical genre– to situate it in a wider cultural context.

There is no longer any place for images divorced from the conditions of their production, considered as aesthetic products pigeonholed according to some label or other rather than as what they really sig-nify from a socio-cultural point of view.

We will only have a history of photography that genuinely contributes to the sum of human knowledge when we have learned to reflect in the necessary depth on the uses and applications that have been made of the photographic image in the course of history. And in addition to this, we will then understand that in both stages, both in the elab-oration of the image (the moment of its conception/ construction/ materialization by the photographer addressing the subject) and in the subsequent trajectory of this image in time and space (as it is appreciated, interpreted and felt by different observers), whatever the object represented may happen to be, there always has been and will continue to be a complex and fascinating *process of construction of realities* and thus of *fictions*. This is an interesting angle from which to reevaluate history.

With the progress of digital technology, the images of the world are equally bound up with the wonderful and the terrible, according to the uses and applications they are put. Who is concerned about the ethical issue that all of this raises? **As the software becomes more and more sophisticated, history will be transformed into advertising,** and the historical memory into synthetic memory, cloned memory, devoid of life, for all that it may be iconographically *true*: It is the triumph of the representation over the datum. What is actually new about this new situation in relation to the past? *Only a refinement of the process of creation/ construction of realities, the real goal of photography.*

Boris Kossoy, is a historian, photographer, archltect and essayist and former director of the Museum of sound and image in Sao Paolo.

* Los temas aquí tratados fueron discutidos y profundizados en mis trabajos: *Fotografia e História*, São Paulo: Editora Ática, 1989 (la editorial La Marca de Buenos Aires está preparando una versión del libro en español); *Realidades e ficções na trama fotográfica*, São Paulo, Ateliê Editorial, 1999; y en el artículo "La fotografía en Latinoamérica en el siglo XIX: la experiencia europea y la experiencia exótica", en: *Image and Memory, photography from Latin America 1866-1994*, Houston Texas University Press, 1998, y en otros textos.

Cabe recordar aquí algunas antologías como la *History of Photography*, lanzada en 1976 y que fue dirigida por Heinz Henisch durante 14 años. Esa revista si, por un lado, publicaba temas bastante convencionales, por otro, abrió un espacio para que el público especializado tomase contacto con la historia de la fotografía en países del Este europeo, asiáticos, latinoamericanos, hecho inédito en las publicaciones de la época. De los primeros años de la década de los 80 es la *Rivista di storia e critica della fotografia*, dirigida por Angelo Schwarz y que, lamentablemente, sólo llegó hasta el sexto número. Otra antología que se debe mencionar es la mejicana *Luna Córnea*, publicada por el Centro de la Imagen y que fue dirigida inicialmente por Pablo Ortiz Monasterio, y actualmente por Patricia Gola.

WRITING HISTORY
"OPENING THE CRACKS"

Mounira Khémir

The text that follows is divided into two parts. The beginning is a testimony that draws upon my work in the fields of research and writing. This is followed by an analysis of how this examination ties in with the questions of methodology that are raised by the writing of the history of photography. The research concerns a geographical area called the "Orient" at a time when this history was being born, namely, the 19th Century.

Long before photography was discovered, the history of art and more specifically the history of works of art, was above all a history of authors, whether they were painters, sculptors or anything else. This bias influenced the writing of the history of photography, despite the lack of reliable monographs on the most significant authors. But what happens in this discipline when the subject broached is that of early photography, a term that mainly encompasses the 19th Century? Which authors, or more precisely, which operators are we dealing with? Are they merely names in the registers? Should the type of history that is like a shrine to the great masters be upheld, or should it be superseded so that the history of photography may become a history of representations? There is, moreover, a link between its specificity and the stakes that this medium implies: the history of forms and the history of uses, in Henri Focillon's words, are related.

Thus, the link I established in the history of forms between Orientalism, a 19th Century pictorial movement, and photography produced by those who travelled to the East or installed studios there, shows that fiction dies hard. [1] Perhaps the peculiarity of the photograph is that it is not a virtual image. It shows the one and only configuration that was possible at that precise moment in time. The image, the metaphor and the analogy were at work very early on in this type of representation. There is no need to emphasise how photographs helped to renew the painter's vision, and not only among the Orientalists. Thus, in the worst cases, the Orientalist painting that is a copy of a photograph, may be seen as a deformation of a deformation. An image deformed but above all, an image transformed. Images of images raise the question of the precarious nature of the image and especially the ambivalence of certain symbolisms. The question of resemblance is no longer in the thing that is perceived but in the eye which perceives it. Moreover, the links between the colonised and the colonisers which prompted "indigenous" photographers to follow in the wake of European photographers shows, as the Arabic sociologist Ibn Khaldoun had already pointed out in the 14 th Century, that the vanquished often adopt the customs and habits of the vanquishers.

The total rejection of any image that was not produced within the local context (at the end of the 19 th Century in Algeria) is also a way of showing that this fiction was a reality and that it must be treated as such. The relation is particularly troubling in the case of photography. As a medium invented by Europeans, the photograph points to the conditions of its production. Although this is necessary

1 I am referring here to my work on Orientalism and the following are the two main publications which accompanied exhibitions:
L'Orientalisme, l'Orient des Photographes, Photopoche n° 58, Paris, Centre National de la Photographie.
Orientalism, Delacroix to Klee, The Art Gallery of New South Wales, Sidney, 1997.

it is not at all diminishing because photography is also a history of meetings and exchanges, even if they are violent on the symbolic level. This heritage increasingly calls for an examination by African and Arabic countries of how they perceive themselves.

Very early on in this history, the photograph gave people access to legendary towns and cities. The Orient, as a destination, remained somewhat vague, even if a corpus of photographs was linked to it. Before the present divisions of Eastern Europe, the Middle East and the Far East, this vast and ill-determined Orient was already taking on different colours when it came to colonial Algeria and the other colonies. Which gave rise to the name used in the archives of certain museums (Colonial nudes). [2] Indeed, a great many gateways led to the East. That they stretched from Venice to Samarcand is a detail which also belongs to a topography, linked, in the best of cases, to a positive fiction.

However, we can only be puzzled when faced with the multiple ''scenes and types'' of anonymous pictures. [3] The gash left by naming is so deep that any consistency lies precisely in inconsistency and in the power of the imagination. What these images reveal is already the West's own confession of itself. They are a materialisation and a man-

2 See the *Photopoche* text , Orientalisme, op.cit.

3 An initial inventory of photographic collections of the Maghreb and the Middle East, compiled after research work that I was granted by the Institut du Monde Arabe, only interested Robert Delpire , who was, at that time, the Director of the Centre National de la Photographie.

ifestation of signs.[4] But even if we disagree with these images, what can be used as an aid for producing other definitions, and in retaliation to what? It must be said that the colonialists' pictures induce a certain passivity. The relation between the text and the image began, generally speaking, with the colonialist novel. What is often forgotten is the intrinsically diminishing side of photography and the problem that as a trace, the photograph shows what has been but is no more. How poor these photographs are, as far as the imagination is concerned, must also be emphasised and the recreational and emotional aspects, which were conducive to their existence, must not be forgotten either. Many of the photographers fell in love with these countries and their landscapes.

Despite the growing interest for this Orient, that music and fashion have made popular again, the archives have remained silent. This has certainly been the case since I first raised the question, in several publications, of what the example-type may be, of Egypt for instance. Of the close link between Egypt and the history of photography and yet the lack, until very recently, of any related publication, despite the massive production of photographs taken there. Of the immediate link between the discovery of photography and Egyptology, since Arago's memorable declaration before the members of the *Institut*

4 Although an Algerian writer had published *Le harem colonial* the Musée Nièpce in Chalons Sur Saône, France, classified certain photographs as "Colonial Nudes". We are dealing here with different places in which history is produced.

de France : "To copy the thousands of hieroglyphs that cover the walls, inside and out, of the grandest monuments in Thebes, Memphis, Karnak and so on, would take several decades and a whole legion of draughtsmen. With the daguerreotype, this enormous task can be carried out by a single man."[5]

Such a scheme seems quite neat and tidy. All it does is to reiterate the fundamental issues that Michel de Certeau exposed in his book "L'écriture de l'histoire".

Indeed, can we talk about an historical institution with regard to the history of photography? What about the essential work of identifying the country or countries and the people or peoples? As a brief example of this, whatever the cultural similarities between the countries of the Maghreb, it is always shocking for a native of one of these countries to see how, in the various publications that rely on pictures, such as the holiday guides of certain prestigious companies, the three are rolled into one.

This writing is not one of the written or spoken text, but of the image and the word. The lack of conjunction implies, at first, that the value of this writing is non-associative. The space given over to the text is often very limited or is only there to attract the type of writer whose prestige will help to sell a book of photographs that is expensive to produce and not easy to sell. Given that such phenomena exist, we have on the one hand what are called coffee-table books and on

5 François Arago, le daguerréotype, a report delivered to the *Académie de Sciences, Paris, on August 19, 1839,* ed. L'échoppe, Caen, 1987.

the other university papers that are only just beginning to appear and are never even published. In a country such as France, there are many outlets and institutions for photography that have become references in the matter and yet there is a chronic shortage of research tools for the history of photography. A terrible lack indeed. The initiative of the group "*Etudes photographiques*" which took over *La Société Française de Photographie* must be stressed, but how open they are to younger researchers from further afield remains to be seen. Perhaps the question of the writing of the history of photography is envisaged according to certain priorities, in which case the ground has already been cleared.

On the other hand, the status of object that the photographic image has had since its beginnings, gives us leave to wonder why the stamp of certain institutions, such as the Bibliothèque Nationale or the Arts-décoratifs, is right in the middle of the picture, spoiling what is sometimes a unique print. At the start of this history, the question was doubtlessly one of the object and of heritage. Indeed, the image is primarily a part of a heritage that must be conserved. This point is very important, but to what degree is it carried out to the detriment of other aspects, such as the funds necessary for research?

Such photography, as a spectacle of the world, was cut off from its immediate referent. Early on, with the work "*Excursions daguerriennes*"[6] the world was seen from one place i.e. France. The question of place is of utmost importance because, as a means to understanding, it addresses each and every one of us and at the same time belongs

6 Excursions daguériennes published by Lerebours from 1841 to 1844.

to several different disciplines. Indeed, asking where the picture is taken from is the same as querying where we speak from and where we write history from. These are the only questions that are liable to help to open the "cracks" with regard to such writing. Again and again they raise the question of scriptorial force and the need to involve "Orientals" in the writing of history. But despite its scriptorial force, writing is always under the threat of being annuled by the power of the image itself.

The exhibition as a phenomenon: to exhibit photographs is, in a way, to give preponderance to the image that celebrates the very process of exhibition. The text, whatever its content, is relegated to second place. The visibility of the image is so strong, so blatant, that the text almost becomes a blind spot, existing by disjunction rather than by association in the construction of meaning. These photographs, as traces of a given period within a wider historical context, incorporate the historical ties relative to their production. But the text is always secondary and, in photographic circles at least, this leads to questions such as: "Who reads it anyway?" It seems to me that we are heading towards a time when the image, as a fragment, could almost have the presence of the sign. A sign so visible that it will inevitably be put into words. At a time when optimism is out of place, a return to the text seems to me to be almost essential. "Return" is only a way of expressing the desire for transparency and the crystal clear myth that haunts the West and accompanies the proliferation and flow of images in which everything "must" go through the same portal. A metaphor of no small moment. Today the West is the defender of the visible, the imaginable and the transportable.

Writing history and the place or the postulate that interpretation is constructed from a particular place and in the present, and the question of the authors' perspicacity and inadequacies, requires that the field be reconsidered in order to organise the representations and to offer reinterpretation. This questioning should come under the heading of an archaeology of visual perception in Foucault's sense. The question of the production of images linked to a reduction-abstraction. Which raises the question of a society that Michel de Certeau calls "scriptorial" insofar as it is confronted by a world of pictures: paste and copy. But without evoking Clément Roussel and the subject of the double, the visible can always be described as something else. It is more than a practice that has "the value of scientific model". This practice is not about trying to find some hidden "truth"; it stands as symbol for the very relation between a new breach in time and a modus operandi which produces the kind of "scenarios" that are liable to organise practice into discourse that is comprehensible today – which is, in fact, "writing history".[7] I think that more than searching for the truth, it is a matter of questioning the means used in writing this particular history, namely the history of photography, and of prising open the cracks in order to satisfy the demands that the writing of history requires in general. To work on what is "real" in the photographic representation but is in no way identical to it. What Michel de Certeau calls "The in-between, the situation of history and the problem of reality" is amplified in the writing of the history of pho-

7 Michel de Certeau, L'Ecriture de l'histoire, Paris, Gallimard, 1975.

tography. Indeed, the sign of history is not so much what is real as what is intelligible. Opening the cracks would be a way of avoiding what is often a collision with the intelligible.

"R. Barthes draws a parallel between "the prestige of having happened" and the current development of the realist novel, the diary, the daily news, the museum, photography, documentaries etc. Each discourse is one of a lost (past) *reality*; each brings a reality that was exiled from language back into the confines of a text, like a relic."[8]

But in addition to the question of history as myth, is that of the Orient as place of myths and subsequent legends, in other words, primarily as a place of the imaginary. Only work on the delimitation of the place, time and space and therefore on the particular, would allow "historical" credibility to emerge with all the caution that should characterise an enterprise such as the writing of the history of photography. "Representation... the literary dramatization, is only "historical" if it is linked to a *social space* of scientific operation and if it is joined, both institutionally and technically, to a *practice of detachment* in relation to contemporary cultural and theoretical models..."[9]

"The word *history* vacillates between two extremes : a narrative that is recounted (story) and actual events (Geschichte). This idea may be hackneyed but it has the merit of pointing, between the two meanings, to a space in which work and mutation are possible. Because the historian always begins with the former and aims at the latter in

8 Michel de Certeau, op. cit. p 55.
9 Michel de Certeau, op. cit. p 101.

order to prise open a crack between the lines of culture that will reveal something that happened elsewhere and in another way. In this sense, (s)he *produces* history." [10]

The idea of "orientalism" means replacing the system of representation deformed by space with a space that would allow us, as a people, to write our own history. A people that does not participate in the production of images that are representations does not write its own history. In the same way that the Carolingien manuscripts conveyed one vision of the world, photographs transmit another. A collection or corpus of photographs in isolation does not stand for all the photographs taken. The will to compose requires the intelligence of an eye that is attentive to alterities.

One question remains nonetheless: should the writing of the history of photography be closed or open when the corpus itself is open?

I will close with an anecdote that came up recently. While I was working at the Cartier Foundation on the theme of the desert, the figure of Lawrence of Arabia arose. Subsequently, I discovered the photographs he took that are conserved in the Ashmoleon Museum in Oxford. My reaction, at a work meeting, was to say that they were pictures of Djeddah, that he took pictures of the architecture, of the mineral as it were and did not photograph the desert because he "lived" it. In saying this, I saw the connection between a global vision of the desert as a place, and somewhere or other, the retreat as the major figure in this representation: the photographers' dissatisfac-

10 Michel de Certeau, op. cit. p 291.

tion when they try to bring out the plasticity of the desert and the apprehension experienced by the first photographers who stood before it. One of the people at the meeting then asked "But how do you know he didn't take any pictures of the desert?". This comment plunges us into the very heart of the matter. The question of interpretation when faced with an open corpus and the meaning we construct from documents. To write and remain attentive to a wider history is perhaps to give relief to the surface of the photograph. [11]

Mounira Khémir, is an art critic and curator.

[11] Exhibition at the Cartier Foundation, Paris from June-September 2000, comprising a large number of early photographs on the theme of the desert.

UNCOMFORTABLE REFLECTIONS
Teresa Siza

None of these things is of any importance. They are like everything else in the ordinary run of life, a dream of the mysteries and the battlements, and I contemplate, like a herald arrived, the plain of my meditation.

That is Fernando Pessoa –or Bernardo Soares– in the *Livro de Desinquietação*. And it is also –I cannot leave him out– Jorge Molder in any of his photographic series in which he **does not** portray himself. Here are the two of them again: *Then we also have our night, and the tiredness of all the emotions is made deeper still by their being emotions of thought, already deep in themselves. But it is night without rest, without a moon, without stars, a night as if everything had been turned inside out – the infinite become interior and dense, the day become the black lining of an unknown suit.*

Jorge Molder and the irresistible evocation of Fernando Pessoa, 'estranged' gazes turned on a mode of presentation of the impossible truth, a truth that must, by definition, be transparent.

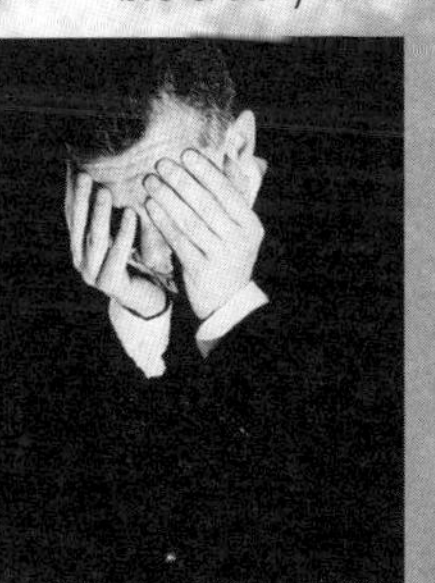
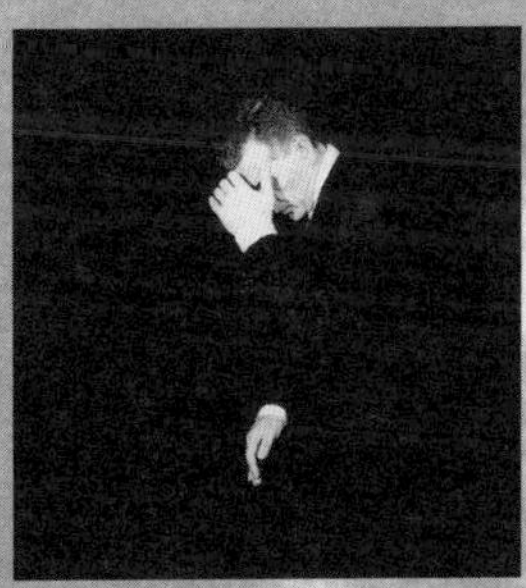
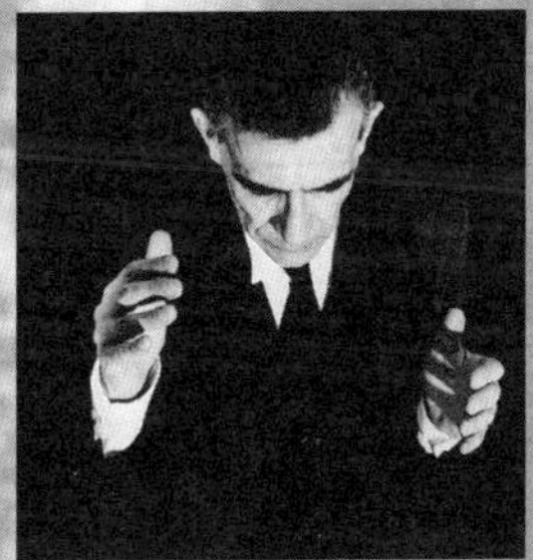

Jorge Molder, untitled, 1997

We are still living in the age of the 'psychoanalysis of the image', in parallel with an *empire of signs*, with its retinue of reified ideals, as Fontcuberta has it. We have made of the plane surfaces that are effects of technological mechanisms returning mirrors and time machines. Out of a spontaneous feeling of the world, albeit with a sensory and linguistic matrix, out of that experience in action we have constituted concepts and intellectual proofs with a savour of the paradigm.

The photographic image is dominated by the 'presence effect' which, no being perception, *inhabits the gaze*, (Fernando Gil). Without presence —even if this be a super-reality in the form of the sensible— there is no art. The gaze is inhabited by other clandestine presences, formal, historical, ideological, social; there is always superimposing of registers in the analysis of an image.

Some of these registers are far from universalist, forming part of a very personal experience of the subject who looks. Like my irresistible evocation of Fernando Pessoa on looking at Jorge Molder's technically perfect, rationally calculated images. As for certainties, I can arrive at some: these are images measuring 120 x 120 cm, silver iodide gelatine, produced in 1997.

The history of the photographic image is not necessarily the history of photography. We can reduce it to its technical, chemical or digital characteristics and those of the support, attribute to it formal elements of style, especially on the basis of technical effects associated with certain artistic currents, we can undertake a brief analysis of content, fundamentally taking into account present perspectives on second analyses. A history of the photographic image is indispensable for describing the evolution –or regression– in the use of materials and technologies, the relationship with scientific and technological vectors in development parallel, its application in the various fields of social intervention, the cultural complex in which it can be included. A museum of the image, identical in information, makes perfect sense.

Very few of these indications respond to the reasons that led me to establish an identification between a complex poet and a difficult photographer. In the tangle of motives and conditions of production of these images these are points of departure and never points of arrival.

If a history of the image is indispensable for our obsessive taxonomies, a history of photography, being necessary, imposes other reflections, other polemical interpretations.

Walter Benjamin observed that photography introduced a revolutionary new artistic practice, given that it freed the hand –traditionally the auxiliary of the creative process– by transferring the 'modelling' of the work to the photographer's eye. Photography is first and foremost a technique of reproduction and framing rather than a gaze. A gaze that is situated, informed, loaded with emotion and culture – a certain culture, a dated sensibility.

The mechanism of photography is culturally coded, and those cultural codes that are inscribed within it include the breaks and continuities, the dreams and desires of the avant-gardes, the aesthetic conformity of the followers, in a word, all the formalisms.

To capture these, to address the explanation of the sensation it arouses in us, calls for a configuration of the history of mentalities: Pictorialism can be explained in terms of both the identity of purposes that were to produce a New Art and of the aristocratic, élitist camp that reacted against the cheapening of art through its technical reproducibility.

It represents a new universe of myths (from Salomé to Orpheus, in the analysis of Gilbert Durand) to set against the myths of Prometheus and Icarus, framing the ideal of progress of 19th-century industrial globalization. It is this disqualified, marginalized fringe in the era of the nationalist engineers –the dandy, the 'damned' artist, the decadent, the mystic, but also the emancipated woman and the anarchist– that took its place on the stage for the creation of the society of the mass-media and high-speed communication.

It is the time of the triumph of the middle classes, which took the place in the objectives and orentations of power of the civil society of liberalism. The Modern Movement had to take due account of the new culture, its network of communication and distribution, the cultural pattern of the altered biorhythm.

A technical and artistic product, at once craft-based and technological, photography is profoundly immersed in the accumulation of gestures and cultures and at the same time, in its role as a mirror substitute, in the formulation of a supremely liberal

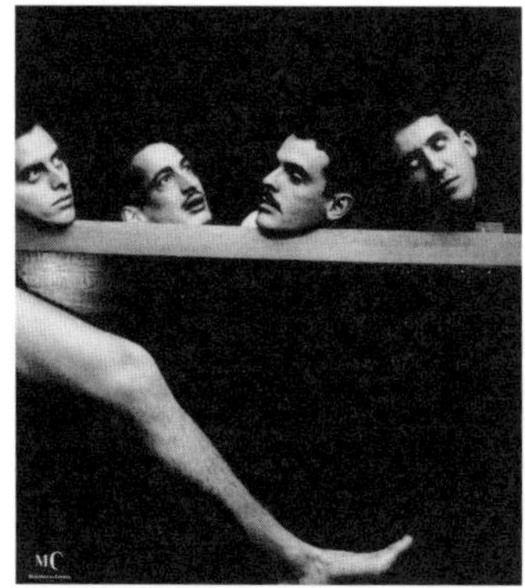

Thomas Farkas, untitled

image of itself that has powerful matrices in the myth and in the metaphysics of the subject. A history of a technique that puts forward modes of representation that are anchored in aesthetic movements, even if these are personalized by the photographers themselves, does not provide for what a history of a medium of this kind requires: namely the explanation of the moments of fracture, the periods of repetition and development of the adaptation of techniques and currents to objectives, the periods of normalization of such fractures, the flows of change that traverse the social dimension and are the driving force behind the creation of new paradigms.

The techniques and the technologies, especially in a world of accelerated appropriation dominated by state-of-the-art techniques, constitute a network of uses that render the singular application non-signifying and empty of content. For the rest, is in the realms of the greatest diffusion of photography –in advertising, in mass communication– that successive technical innovations make the most immediate impact. And these two aspects belong fundamentally to a history of the images, independently of the fact that in many cases photographers and images may participate in a history of photography that includes the movement of ideas and feeling.

Photographic images are more and more a source of epistemological reflection, mirroring with greater or lesser intensity ideological movements or interiorizations, representations of the social whole and its parts, and aesthetic, ethnic or specifically cultural attitudes. Everything points towards an increase in the use of the photographic imaginary in the engagement with history – in globalizing, sectorial or monographic perspectives and in epistemological study.

Treated as a documentary source they offer a notable enrichment of the interpretation of history, of the analysis of society and of aesthetic movements. With the increasing computerization of the knowledge at our disposal –the whole digitalized medium tends to constitute stocks of information for consultation 'timings' controlled by the user– and the necessary rationalization of 'navigation' in the information networks, there is an inevitable diminishing of the data content, progressively fragmenting and regionalizing the blocks of information. With such an information deficit –already perfectly evident in the pressurizing of digital information– what we will see emerging are 'sectorial histories' of photography: a history of the technique, a history of the photographic aesthetic (or autonomy), a social history, an ideological history. And at the same time the photographic image will also be present in the countless complementary sciences or arts.

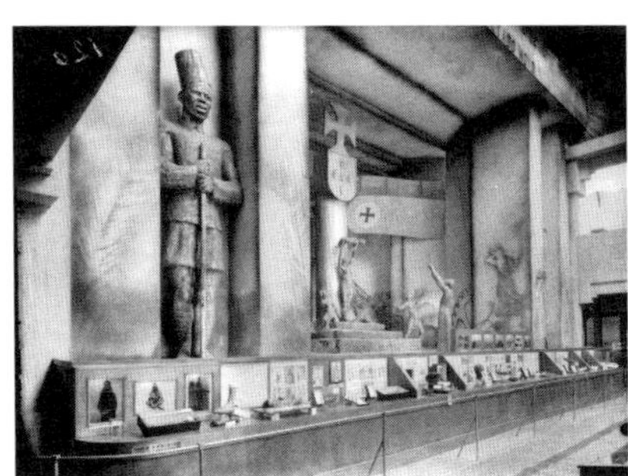 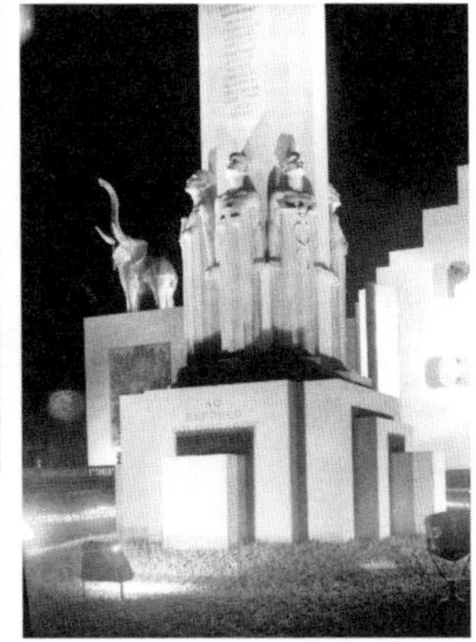

It is quite clear that photography articulates history, but history not only informs the photographer, it also clarifies the understanding of the photographic image and of its history.

The photography produced by minorities now appears quite automatically on the information 'highways', as a natural appropriation of a space of presence. This has always been true of all the arts, which strive to be as universal as possible. Photographers representing minorities, whether ethnic or social, have overcome through the value of their work the obstacles that always seem to beset difference. The great innovation of the information highways –and digital television will make the circulation of the world's stock of information still more accessible– is precisely the irruption, the presence. of minorities of every kind, of representations of what is still known as the Third World or disadvantaged or awkward groups, such as AIDS sufferers. Which makes it possible to admit that that problem will soon cease to be a problem. A history of images with an archaeological basis will have to take into account the ideological vision and 'the gaze of the other' in exactly the way that anthropology has to do.

There is a belief that the contemporary photographic testimony reveals itself as belonging to the community as a whole, but it tends to an ever greater subjectivity, open to the broad understanding of ethnic, social and cultural differences. From the moment that Photography comes to be based on a subjective attitude it also opens itself up to art and it is through art that alterity can be affirmed, reflecting the cultural hybrids that are opening up in the world; in all the world and more and more all the time, with the circulation of people in geographical space and through the channels of communication.

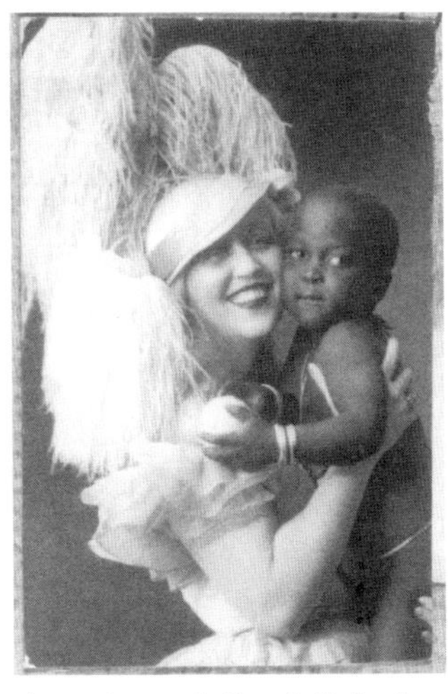

The photographs of Keita reflect the way that Africans were represented in the European imaginary, but at the same time it is easy to detect the exclusive harmony of the patterns and the specifically African use of the image to show lineage.

These analyses do not take account of two affirmative aspects of the photography of the last 30 years: its militant adoption —in terms of what this means in a period when individualism has ceased be Romantic and liberal— of postmodernism and the tendency towards the digital adventure also, and especially, in photography (it is a well known fact that in Europe in particular the learning of digital technology is taking place in the schools of sound engineering and photography, and far less in the film and television schools). The anchor of the old philosophy of the subject is now notoriously divided into two currents, that of the philosophy of the system, which claims to be able to do away with the tension between society and individual/ cultural agent, and a pragmatic current which postulates the existence of a communicational and critical reason that enables the pragmatic control of reality by means of a rational consensus within diversity and complexity. It is a matter, of course, of two different bids to maintain the beliefs of Modernity; under their direction the critique of postmodernism has been concomitant with the development of the strategies that formed it as strategies of militancy. And it is also by means of them that these have been transcended, attentive to the theoretical void that was seen to lie at the basis of postmodernist practices.

And among other things, photography has come to be regarded, from the 70s on, as the privileged and naturally predisposed medium, as the fragmentary and silent object that sets out to reconstruct a global totality of the world and a language for the critique of postmodernism.

And computers should be seen as a key structural element of this culture of transition towards the 21st century, in which a variety of pundits have asserted the end of history and the end of human progress. Computer games, cyberspace and virtual reality are evident and powerful ramifications of that culture – a culture of the present, ahistorical, and one that claims to be the ideal of progress, an affirmation of the power of the few over the many.

That the evolution of culture and society is diverging from the forecasts drawn up by the masters of power can be seen in the fact that the computer was launched onto the American market in order to wrest from the workers the control they still exercised over the processes of production.

In postmodern culture the subject is decentred. The fragmentation of identity –which is clearly reflected in photography– is a product of the dispersion and loss of the whole centre. In regarding itself as ahistorical, postmodern culture, *that pure screen and system of empty signs* (Marga Clark), cannot conceal our ever greater and more urgent need for our (own) history to be told.

The existence of a social subject is still, in this age in which even the fixed signal-referent relationship has been altered, a condition of survival. We still give names to things so as not to lose ourselves in the

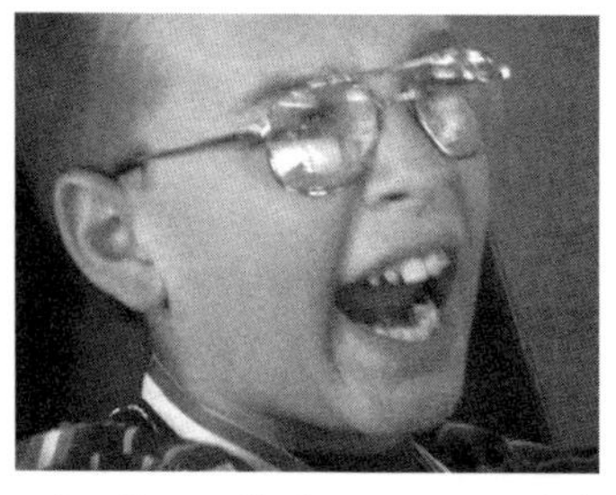

world. And the postmodern movement, which boasted it would combat social and ethnic hierarchies and differentiation, has failed to bring about the triumph of popular culture – a culture that is based on the relationship with nature. The predominance of technological cal culture –that guarantee of the existence of a technological unconscious that secretes a new cultural skin– made it possible, with the development of the mass-media and the spread of the digital media, for individuals to shut themselves away: the technologies are evolving in the sense of allowing human beings to stay at home. The home now is a true place of refuge, in which all the appliances and gadgets serve to ensure the connection with a less and less concrete world, in which the pictures of experience are produced in aseptic conditions, carefully isolated from pernicious contacts.

This ramification of electronic technology leads to the elimination of conventional notions of space, time and place. In this context, words such as 'exploitation' and 'social class' have no meaning or are simply not relevant, but that appearance of democracy is no guarantee of a concern with social justice; there is no social class, there are only individuals in a universe in which what counts are individual experiences, based on an unconsidered right to be informed and to feel. Space is the space of the screen, the journey takes place in the space of the data-communication highways or in cyberspace, the struggles are computer simulations. The new activists of our world are digital intervention groups operating on the Internet under dehumanized names such as 'Circle of Mars', 'Spectral Force', 'Sabre' and other virtual realities.

A present that is eternalized, consumption and leisure as spectacle; in its latest process of consumption of the world in the form of images, it subsists in the digital world in an increasingly phantasmagoric fashion.

The principal creative strategies of postmodernism –fundamentally critical, ironic and distanced, as we all know– are concerned with cultural stereotypes and, above all else, with the medium of photography as aesthetic experience. They accentuate the imperfections of the images they appropriate, putting themselves forward as re-photographs in which the relationship with the real has been lost and a dialogue with the image introduced in its place.

We have all seen how well the postmodern photographers sell, how their images, which have invented a new meaning for photographic production, arouse the interest of museums and collectors who are prepared to fight to acquire them, negating the objective principal of the critique, the struggle against the art market and the concept of value of the photographic work and of the photographer. Secreting an intransigent morality, postmodernism shut itself up in a codified system of self-consumption. Nevertheless, it renewed the art of photography and resituated it in the realm of self-interrogation.

Once again we find photography, that fragile and bereft object, *that minimum layer in which reality lives* (Lemagny), in search of itself, because it has been unable –and is powerless– to force the course of things. And because it has proved incapable of altering the course of culture and imposing its choice of alternatives, its initial purpose from 1970 on, it continues to be a very specific art whose destiny seems to present itself as a concentric movement always in the interior of the same old questions. Continually placing itself in doubt, it sets about inventing itself in successive representations, while the alterity and with it the eternal seduction of Photography remain. As an art it can confront the subject with a presence, in a process that resists any kind of intellectualization. A rhetoric of spontaneity and sentimentality, it embraces an understanding of its poetic dimension – the tension between the legacy of the Beaux Arts tradition (the poetics of form) and that of literature (the poetics of time). Repeating the problem-questions over the course of time, photography's responses constantly diverge on the basis of the cultural context, of the conflicts and breaks it adopts as its own. As a history of desire, like every product of the human spirit, it navigates in the irreducibility of the rhetoric of the psychoanalytical unconscious to the rhetoric of the technological unconscious. It is a complex object which invites many different readings, and can only be explained in terms of the demands that each age places on it. It has been and is the mirror of Narcissus. The image offers man a mirror in which to project part of himself. But Narcissus has moved on. It was man who oriented the whole sum of psychic energy towards his own image, lacking a social and public dimension. The world was the mirror in which

Narcissus saw himself; these days it is in the universe of images that the world —the global Narcissus, its body dissolved in external entities of a technical imaginary— contemplates itself.
Never has a contextualized history of photography been so necessary as it is now.

Teresa Siza, Director of the Centro Portugués de Fotografía

Joan Naranjo

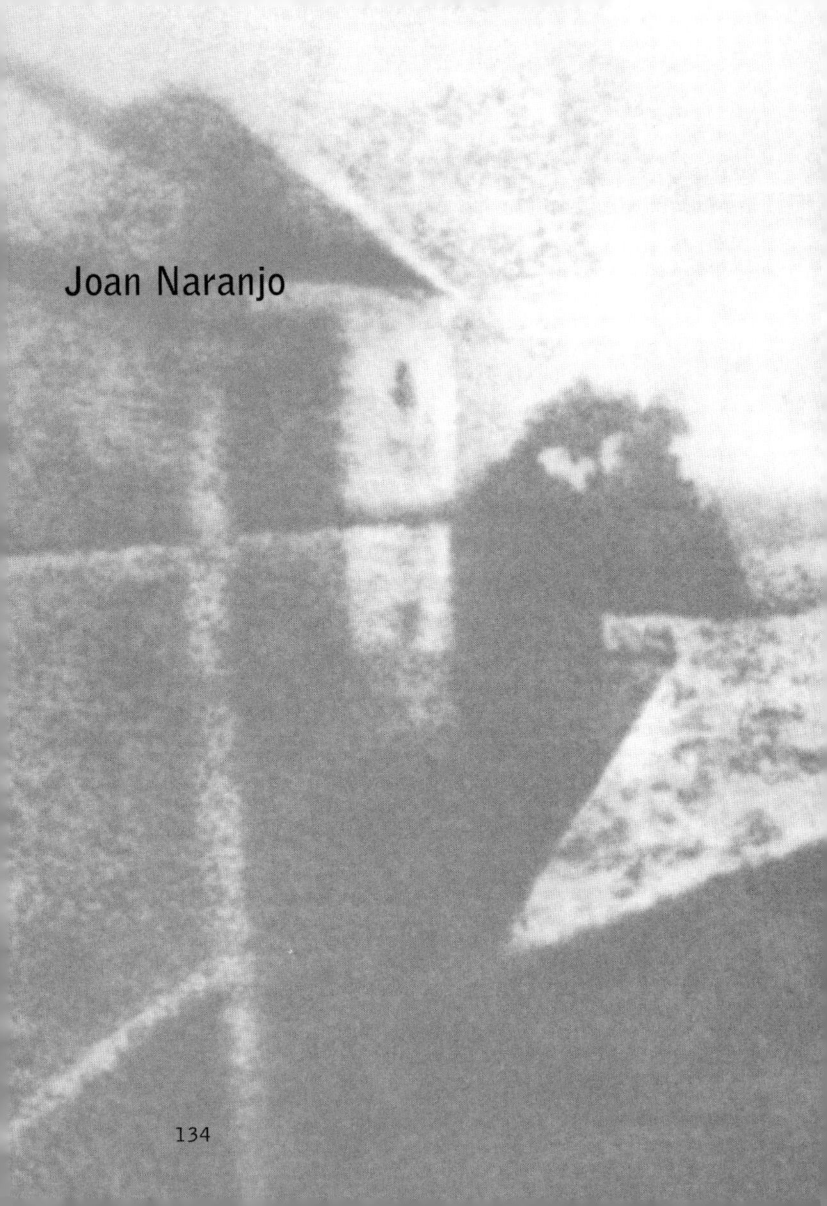

The last twenty or thirty years have seen a significant increase in photography-related publications: monographs, historical studies, essays, biographies, autobiographies, analyses of particular periods or genres, compilations of texts, etc. All of this intense activity in relation to photography has provided us with a rich and extensive inventory of images and contexts.

This output has been far from even, and not always very enlightening. There was no significant change in the studies of the history of photography until the publication of the *Nouvelle Histoire de la Photographie*, edited by Michel Frizot[1]. This is one of the first histories of photography to break with the single-author principle in favour of offering the broader vision of a large number of writers, renovating the habitual iconographic repertoire in this type of publication and introducing photographs by creative talents from countries which have been consigned to pigeon-holes — neglected — on the fringes of photographic history, as is the case of Spain. The visual discourse of this book is of considerable importance, and ties in with the actual uses and functions of photography.

A large part of this significant volume of material belongs more to the domain of archaeology than to that of history, if by archaeology we mean the recovery of material and data in a way that is acritical and 'objective'. Of course, any process of selection is subjective, even when the data is not analysed in the same way as it would be by a historian. This may be a very obvious idea, but it is

1 Michel Frizot, (ed.), *Nouvelle Histoire de la Photographie*, París: Bordas, 1994

important to clarify the position here so as not to enter into contradiction when using the word 'real', but taking this word instead in a much broader and more metaphorical sense. There is indeed a 'real' history of photography, or rather, a series of 'real' histories of photography, given that different points of view and approaches have served to open up new lines of research and of interrelations between disciplines in which social, aesthetic, technological and, more recently, cultural aspects have been worked with. The sum of all these contributions is what configures the map of knowledge that allows us to come closer to an understanding of photography, its engagements with other disciplines, and its history.

The current state of play on the international scene is not applicable to the same degree in our country, given that our situation, in essence, is not so different from what it was in 1988 when Joan Foncuberta was calling for a change in attitude to the history of photography in this country: 'The challenge facing photohistorians, then, is not so much the quest for data, but rather precisely that of the creation of a set of criteria of evaluation and the subsequent application of these. It follows that the archaeologist of photography can no longer limit his role to that of an acritical "excavator" – he must take on this same critical dimension'[2]. It is true that there have been changes which have been reflected in a significant volume of publishing activity and in the introduction of photography in the academic world – first in the universities and now at the secondary-school level. But

2 Joan Fontcuberta, "Crítica y nuevas tendencias" en VVAA, *La crítica fotográfica*, Durango: Museo de Arte e Historia, 1988.

the historical focus – which has conserved a fair degree of the archaeological – remains largely unchanged. The official histories are
content merely to recover the memory of a historical and photographic heritage within a 'social' context, very often obviating the
platforms for diffusion and reception of photographs, their multiple applications, the impact photography had on the scientific discourse of the 19th century and its pedagogical repercussions, especially in the teaching of art, in society and in the way of perceiving
the world and 'reality'.

Let us hope that this symposium will serve to open up new ways of
approaching a more general awareness of the history of photography, and to consolidate the various initiatives in this line which
have emerged to date and which are perhaps being generated at
the moment.

There is a need to undertake a revision of some of the models of selection employed up until now. These have to a large extent maintained previously established norms, and there is no re-reading of the
images. This conformism is based on the creation of two categories: high photography and low photography.

High photography encompasses those images which, thanks to their
reproduction in numerous books of photographic history over almost
a century now, have become pieces with a high economic value, and
have come to form part of the collections of major museums,
which also makes them part of the élite of photographic culture, or
of photographic 'art'.

Low photography is made up of a series of images in formats
which generally do not have economic value in the photographic mar-

ket, such as visiting cards–,[3] which have often been looked down upon by many historians who consider this type of photograph as belonging to the photographic industry rather than to the 'art' of photography. In many cases, these are anonymous images or are the product of countries consigned to the limbo of photographic history. If we compare two photomontages – the first often reproduced, and entitled *Fading Away–*,[4] 1858, by Peter Henri Robinson, and one of the images which go to make up the history of photography, of the history of high photographic culture, and the other an 'untitled' photomontage from circa 1871, produced by the Studio Rovira i Duran, which belongs to low photography, ordinary photography, not regarded as suitable for inclusion in a museum, printed in visiting card format by a photographer of no historical 'relevance' and

3 Newhall escribió en su conocida *Historia de la fotografía, desde sus orígenes hasta nuestros días*, Barcelona: Editorial Gustavo Gili,1983:
"Como retratos, las *cartes de visite* poseen, en su mayor parte un escaso valor estético. No se realizaba ningún esfuerzo para que el carácter de la persona en cuestión apareciera mediante sutileza de iluminación o tras seguir su actitud y su expresión (...). Como documentos de época, tienen a menudo gran encanto e interés. Es a fotógrafos más serios, que trabajaron con formatos mayores, que volvemos a para encontrar los mejores retratos del siglo XIX." Newhall olvida que es gracias a la tarjeta de visita que se produjo una transgresión en los cánones establecidos en el género de retrato. Podemos poner en entredicho su opinión tan reduccionista de "mejores" retratos. ¿Por qué hemos de aceptar que el mejor retrato es el que refleja el espíritu de modelo y no el del creador? ¿Por qué no tener en cuenta los antirretratos o las otras formas de retratar?
4 Newhall, *Ibid.* sitúa este fotomontaje en su capítulo "Fotografía y arte".

produced in a country banished to the fringes of the history of photography – we can see that the photomontage by the Studio Rovira i Duran is really more valid than Robinson's, by virtue of its innovative and ground-breaking character which sets it apart from the work of its time and makes it part of the avant-garde. One question which the museum curators and certain photographic historians should ask themselves –or we should ask them– is why images of this sort (low photography) tend to be excluded from the publications of the museum collections and from many books on the history of photography.

The model established by Newhall fails to link up and give a context to photography which goes beyond the formal and aesthetic vision, which seeks to probe the interrelations with medicine, anthropology, architecture, etc., and with the importance of the uses and functions of photography in terms of the cultural history of photography.

Among the most notable failings we might cite here are the preservation of a model which establishes a hierarchy between high and low photography, loaded with aesthetic/formal prejudices, the constant diachronic narrative which fails to relate/address the ways of generating images in different periods, and the ethnocentric vision of photographic history which the historians who have followed this model have handed down to us.

There is no error in leaving out what one is not aware of, but the majority of histories of photography have deliberately omitted the photographic output of almost the entire planet. There may be many reasons for this, but perhaps the most important is that for a long time cultural colonialism weighed heavily in the composition of these studies. In addition to the cultural colonialism and the aesthetic 'élitism' which have tyrannised the process of selecting images carried out by some historians, political conditions have also acted as important filters.

The totalitarianism which reigned over the harshest times in Russia and the countries of Eastern Europe effectively excluded a considerable part of their history, including photography, and the same is true of countries such as Spain. The association of images or their creators with political ideals has been a major cause of historical omission, as in the case of the Italian futurist movement, neglected for a number of years time on account of its association with fascism. Another great filter is the art market, in what is not in is deemed not to exist. Over the last ten years, pictures by photographers from countries such as Russia, the Czech Republic, Poland and Hungary, among others, have won a place in the market, in the history books and in the major collections. This has been possible thanks to the political and cultural opening-up, which created an ideal framework for the revising of the most recent —and forgotten— history, enabling many photographs and photographers to appear both in the market and in the museums of these countries. These changes have also led to the breaking down of certain stereotypes about works and names, and a redefining of certain established concepts, above all those associated with the photography of the period between the wars, copnsigned to the shadows by the official vision of the totalitarian regimes.

 Feedback —between market and history and vice versa— is very important and is one of the factors in the transition from private/unknown photography to public image. We should not forget that interest in the photographic image and, in particular, in its history has evolved along side the photographic market.

Images play a fundamental role in history, in so far as it is they that speak to us; the person who produced them is a further point of reference, enabling us to understand how the images were created. If we analyse a list of photographers whose works we do not know, this data can help us arrive at a statistical vision of, for example, the number of photographers there were in a given city in 1850. At the same time, if we have a collection of images we can formulate a discourse in the absence og any information about the photographer (we are talking about a graphic medium which has to be capable of functioning in its own right) since the form in which we group and contextualise the works will affect the way we see them.

A good example of the dichotomy between author and work can be found in the first decades of photography and in two radically opposed processes. One is the daguerreotype: these are single works, many of which defy ascription, given that they were not usually signed. No large number of daguerreotypes by any one photographer has been conserved. In the daguerreotype process there is a tendency towards standardization on account of technical limitations and the needs of the public for whom they were intended. The result of all this is that, with few exceptions, it is easier to speak of an era and of a way of representing subjects than of the individual character of the photographers. The opposite case is that of the calotype, a process which makes it possible to reproduce the images. In contrast to the daguerreotype, here the character of the creator is predominant, and fairly large volumes of work by individual photographers has been conserved. To the extent that their production responds to criteria different from those of the daguerreotype, here the singularity of the creators is more important.

The relationship between images and photographers (in that order) is what enables us to understand many of the contradictions which arise as we analyse the whole body of work of a photographer, or of an era, especially in the case of the 19th century.

A good method for the study of photography would be to provide a general understanding of photography as a specific topic before going on to apply this to other fields.

'Politically correct' history needs to be integrated into 'real' history, in that there are good reasons for its being 'real', and it is possible for us to do so in an individual work, if not in a general conception of the construction of history. The level of social sensibility at the present time is sufficient to ensure that our historical premisses include minorities, the so-called Third World, etc. The responses to certain problems or questions are always the product of a general situation which affects our way of perceiving, associating and relating, and which has to do with our society, the state of our knowledge and our times.

In the current situation, cultural colonialism has given way to positive discrimination, the results of which can be seen in the publishing of a history of African photography (award-winning, at that), in the reproduction of Spanish photographs in some studies of photographic history, and in the publishing of catalogues such as the *neue Sachlichkeit* and photography in Slovenia – all of which would have been unthinkable until recently.

Although the most 'advanced' countries are the ones which have imposed –and, to a certain extent, continue to impose– their vision of history, it is coming to be the case that previously neglected countries are starting to have a certain specific weight in the 'world-wide' or 'real' history of photography. Where in the past the history of Russian, Czech or Brazilian photography, to name just a few, were not seen as 'important', today almost no one would write a history without mentioning those countries. Let us hope that the creators of historical knowledge go on to adopt more integrationist, less exclusive stances than those which have prevailed until very recently.

The majority of the established criteria for analysing the history of photography have been based on an élitist process of selection, in terms of the relationship between the aesthetic and the formal. The social, technological and cultural contexts have been regarded as secondary, when they have been taken into account at all. I believe that, to a considerable degree, this situation is changing, and this makes it not only compatible but necessary to relate the aesthetic and the social, and to relate uses with forms. If we do not bear in mind the above points, we will not understand the importance of certain works produced for scientific purposes, which are important on the formal as well as on the social and cultural levels.

Joan Naranjo is a historian, collector and director of the Galería Kowasa in Barcelona.

THE FIELD OF DEPTH
Henning Steen Wettendorff

The English 19th-century photographer, P.H. Emerson, published two influential reflections on photography as art; *Naturalistic Photography for Students of the Art* (1889) was followed by the pamphlet *The Death of Naturalistic Photography* only two years later. Both reflected the conceptual and ideological underpinnings of the day. Emerson's change of mind as reflected in the different titles, was essentially motivated by the author's realization that tonal manipulation of the photographic image was limited to expansion or compression of the grey-scale: research by scientists Hurter & Driffield led to photographers' realization of the existence of the density curve - which could be flattened or boosted almost at will, but not exactly overruled. Emerson concluded that such limitations, e.g. the impossibility of swopping tonalities between any two areas in a given image, ultimately made photography insufficient as a medium of art. The work of hand and mind thus proved yet superior to that of the machine, as much as Emerson hated this premature conclusion of his own. 19th-century thought perhaps did not permit him to conclude otherwise.

Today, the digital revolution tends to provoke similar debates in that every pixel of the photographic image is alterable and, in principle, subject to complete manipulation. Only now the situation is the complete opposite: the legitimacy of the image is weakened, implying a reduced potential for any magical realism or even documentary credibility of photography in the digital age. Westonian previsualization is now further undermined by the computer's infinite palette of postvisualization tools, making recent debates about the artificial nature of the photographic image seem like a hammering on not-yet-quite-open doors.

It is the hugely expanded field of options (and some residual machine fear) which now fuels widespread speculation as to whether photo-based artists in the future will tend to prefer the darkroom after all – in order to resume the lost referent, and with it the indexicality and pronounced iconicity pertaining to their medium. Such self imposed limitations of course would make Emerson's reasons for claiming the death of photography as a serious medium seem quite bizarre. On the other hand we're faced with a clear-cut example of the utter importance of changed cultural and techno-logical paradigms framing two historical situations – which leads a surplus of options today to imply (in the eyes of many) a hin-drance to the medium's seriousness, much similar to that implied by Emerson in observing the *lack* of similar options a century ago. Such paradigmatic contradictions are abundant within the short history of the medium, and leaves me seriously wondering as to the whole enterprise of coming to terms with the medium's history in its entirety – especially if performed as that one sweeping gesture implied by volumes such as the *History of Photography*, whether by B. Newhall (1937), by J.M. Eder (1945), by N. Rosenblum (1979), or by J.-Cl. Lemagny and A. Rouillé (1998).[1]

Photography has been applied in a multitude of contexts and is thus likely to change and face the historian with as many possible venues

1 *Histoire de la Photographie* (Paris, 1998).

A similar approach is apparent in *The history of photography from the camera obscura to the beginning of the modern era* (H. and A. Gernsheim, 1969), and in *Die Geschichte der Fotografie im 20. Jahrhundert* (P. Tausk, 1977)

to its meaning and development. The indexical and iconical status of the medium in its classical form further complicates attempts at a comprehensive understanding of the medium in terms of e.g. style, reception, artist biography, technology, semiotics, psychoanalysis, marxism, etc. Reality is omnipresent, if only indirectly, in lens-based photography and must be said to have imposed itself onto many images, especially in street photography, portraiture, journalistic work and other types of images where a human subject could interfere with or at least affect the photographic act itself.

This is not to insist on any ambiguity per sé of the photographic image. Many of the dilemmas and ambiguities facing the historian of the medium are certainly our own mental constructs, our inclination for binary set-ups which simplify any complex field before our eyes. On the contrary, I tend to believe that too many questions about this multifaceted medium are phrased polemically, or generally in terms of dichotomies. Why is it that even Geoffroy Batchen is inclined to identify two base camps consisting of formalists and postmodernists (or "contextualists" in general)? And does the fact that John Szarkowski at MoMA made claims to decontextualize work in some way make a formalistic enterprise (whether artistic or intellectual) less legitimate today?

Binary vision certainly offers the possibility of closing one's eye rather than using both. In enabling "intellectual" binary vision, however, we're not only able to see the missing half, but rather to see the field in its entirety, stretching and in full range and depth. Revisionist historians do not necessarily teach us a different lesson, even if difference certainly increases the intellectual market value of one's ideas. Rather, oeuvres, bodies of work, and even single images assume new, added meaning through these efforts. But such new meaning rarely invalidates previously authoritative or at least dominant interpretations. Nor should they. Of course historians are eager to justify and market their own conclusions, but a substantial argument will always have to make serious attempts toward clarification of its own assumptions, thus enabling the critical reader to substantiate (or overthrow) his own, while simultaneously retaining the full view of potential meaning in sight.

It may seem a neat trick here to market another dichotomy then, and even to have it represent and somehow embrace all other available dualisms on the intellectual market. It would, at any rate, have to be a dichotomy closely linked to the ontology of the photographic image. So it is: *Time* and *Space*. It is almost certainly a distinction which one may discern as a current within, or underneath, most other photography-related notions of antithetical nature (among which the opposition between documentary concern and visual expression is only the most apparent).

Rather than subscribing to Szarkowski's notions in *The Photographer's Eye* (1966), I want to touch briefly on the historical framework discussed by his successor, Peter Galassi (*Before Photography*, 1981); by Geoffroy Batchen Burning with Desire, 1997), and by many others, namely that of the early days of the medium, or even the years preceding the so-called invention of photography in 1839. Rather than practising intellectual oscillation between time and space, *ontologically*, the question would be: is photography primarily bound to time, or to space, *historically*? The spatial projection in the camera obscura and other similar devices of course preceded the fixation of the projected image and therefore renders documentary concerns as secondary to the drive behind representations of three-dimensionality onto flat surfaces, whether for social, scientific, or artistic purposes. As Geoffroy Batchen and others have noted, not even the idea of coating such surfaces with silverhalides and exposing the surfaces to light for a certain amount of time necessarily led 18th-century experimenters to spend all their energy and time on the problem of fixating such intervals to posterity.

Contextualists generally emphasize the camera's early (and late) function as an index-machine, thus linking its products directly to time. Photography in its realized form must have been an incredible and quite unimaginable fusion of the fraction of a second (or minute) with - eternity. Not that smallest fraction of time and that eternal eternity which mathematicians are abstractly concerned with then: on the contrary, time was (and is) easily perceived as a function of nature itself. Even the "duration aspect" of the new medium thus contributed to the way it was felt to be self-generating, easy, magical. Long exposure times only furthered a feeling of light as streaming in through lenses for certain amounts of time and leaving that mark right there on the plates, as if time itself were *the* illuminatory and developing agent for the image, automatically, magically, and invisibly recorded on the plate with the aid of optics, chemistry, and light.

In photographic practice, of course, this dichotomy between time and space may be felt to be overcome, by masters of the medium such as Paul Strand, Henri Cartier-Bresson (who even formed an ideology of "the decisive moment" to occur right on the possible intersection between the two planes), and W. Eugene Smith. The latter keeps confronting me and others with puzzling perplexity which command further scrutiny, perhaps right here and now:

Tomoko is Bathed by her Mother

W. Eugene Smith's (and Aileen Smith's) image "Tomoko is Bathed by her Mother," published e.g. in the book *Minamata* (1975), is an icon of the previous century. It has come to signify the essence of involved humanism in documentary photography; it has been analyzed in terms of its bearings upon generations of reportage photographers, as well as upon the waste policies of a company causing the severe mercury pollution of a bay traditionally feeding its fisherman population; it has been inscribed in a traditional art historical scheme allowing us to discern the "descendence" of religious themes and pictorial schemes in classical painting. It has also been discussed in terms of qualities that pertain to P.H. Emerson's concerns, i.e. the possibilities of manipulating light conditions and tonalities, including the articulation of an expressive photographic language by means of the grey-scale.

Even if Gene Smith has been generally targeted by those historians who have vehemently attacked the liberal tradition of "concerned photography" in the past two decades, "Tomoko is Bathed by her Mother" nonetheless has retained both status and meaning of considerable expanse. This, however, did not prevent the emergence of a very different meaning of "Tomoko" within the first few months of our new century. Let me recall the story in short, as it unfolds day by day on the internet in February and March, even though I suspect that it will already be quite well-known to those interested in photography as they read this. [2]

Regardless of her condition, Tomoko Uemura of course paid a price for acting naked before Smith's camera. So did her family, who never benefited directly from any income that this image may have earned in bookstores, galleries, auctions houses, or at magazine stands; only indirectly, from the general good it may have done to force the Chisso Corp. to change their waste policies in the region. Not bad. Not bad at all. Only, some 25 years later the family cannot help experience bitterness that Tomoko's naked body was to meet the world's eyes for decades, as a consequence of a session where Smith explored angles, moments, light, etc. for more than half an hour (apparently Tomoko Uemura subsequently fell ill from a cold). The family was active in fighting Chisso, and thus saw their daughter and her photograph help bring about real changes: *this photograph made a difference*. Today, however, their pain is evergrowing at every new exposure to the photograph as it is still circulated as an anonymous masterpiece belonging to the canon of documentary photography.

The possible implication that Tomoko in fact suffered from the photographic act performed by the man who was a loving and com-

2 These news was first posted to the *Oracle* mailing list (a curatorial network); then forwarded on February 29th to the History of Photography mailing list (PHOTOHST).

passionate spokesman for her, and for the entire community, is of course depressing – but is presumably not a part of the reason why Aileen Smith decided to transfer all rights to the image to the family.[3] This transfer act, on the other hand, has inspired one of the longest lasting debates on the history of photography mailing list to this day. To contextualist historians these circumstantial aspects of photographic images matter a great deal. So they should. Although negative circumstances for the production (and, possibly, the future reception) of the image does not rule out any positive meaning or artistic value that the image still retains, this particular instance does call for distinctions to be made – a clear stance is necessary by historians and by anybody, as to the claim made by Tomoko Uemura's family decades later that the image now be close to eradicated from public consciousness. Even museums who own a print of the image are asked to transfer it from the display walls to the archives, even if they cannot be forced to do so. Parental guilt may play a role, as only one motivation among a myriad of aspects that can be reason-

3 As moderated by curator Yuko Yamaji of the Kiyosato Museum of Photographic Arts, Japan, the following reasoning appeared on the mailing list: "Although Tomoko died in 1977, the photograph is being exhibited and published constantly. The parents have been in trauma because of the fact that the taking that photograph exhausted Tomoko. She was trembling not only because of the disease but she was feeling uneasy being photographed naked by someone whom she does not know well. The parents finally asked Aileen Mioko Smith, co-copyright holder of the photograph, not to exhibit/publish otherwise they feel that Tomoko's soul can never rest in peace."

152

ably asserted as pertinent to the heated discussion – a discussion which is easily fueled by theories of the (male) gaze and of the victimization that is now widely recognized, at least by the avantgarde within the photographic community itself.

This image made a difference, but did it make a difference by and in itself? Or will the body of work made by Smith when covering this community convey the traumatic aspects and communicate its message equally well without Tomoko in the future. No. Or yes, if adopting a utilitarian stance: the book contains a number of pictures of Tomoko; if only this icon is left out from the next edition of *Minamata*, we're still getting the full sense and rich impression of the scene and the condition of these people at that time. Any talk about art is nonsense, of course, after such a hypothetical crippling of the group of images, but this may be a help rather than a problem to those investigating Smith's legacy.

This was no situation where a subject "affected" the scene through her awareness of the photographer's presence: it was, assumingly, the affection of a photographer who got carried away. As historians, we may get carried away as easily by the fame and photographic qualities of the image. Whereas one has to acknowledge a personal attachment to whatever one chooses for a study, be it even a negative bond, it is nevertheless a historian's task to stay somewhat detached. Valid empathy is mobilized by anyone aiming at the interpretation of significant images – but the empathy should apply to other people's experiences, and in my view empathy is not to be extended to the imagery per sé.

An emotionally powerful image may perhaps "have to" reinsert the historian as viewing subject affected by its inescapable message, at least if one wants to avoid the danger of divorcing oneself from those aspects that are at the heart of what matters in the image. Such calls for phenomenological readings may be extended to any image, of course, but then presents a demand for real self-scrutiny which has to take place on the part of every historian before committing oneself to personal readings of pictorial universes: are such readings based on a belief in phenomenological prescriptions in general, or is it a choice informed by calls from the art industry asking historians to verbalize experience rather than understanding, and thus tune their attitudes in accordance with the growing "infotainment" industry and the development within the museum world toward becoming centers of purchase (of merchandise; food; art, etc.), rather than once-held roles as sanctuary spots.

Henning Steen Wetterdorf is an essayist, critic and editor of the magazine Katalog.

THE MECHANICAL ART: SOME HISTORIC DEBATES ON ART AND PHOTOGRAPHY

Andrea Kunard

The history of photography has never been singular. The medium has been touted as a truthful depiction of events and promoted as a fine art practice. It has been applied to substantiate the theories and beliefs of a wide range of disciplines, and used to present a world of leisure and individual self-fulfilment. Photography is a ubiquitous technology, the study of which cannot be confined to a chronological listing of technical developments and master practitioners. The history of photography is always in the plural, and any analysis must take into account the many factors that have qualified its uses, and the cultural beliefs that have supported such applications.

This essay will examine some of the issues surrounding the entry of photography into the High Art museum. It will begin with the observations of Lady Eastlake who contended that the photograph, because of its verisimilitude, could never attain the status of a fine art. Over a century later, Clement Greenberg argued the exact opposite; photography achieved its artistry through the frankness of its depictions of the world. Both beliefs betray the desire to explain the relationship between the mechanical and spiritual; there is a need to either accept or disparage the idea that spirit could find expression through technology. These arguments in turn express the persistent Eurocentric preoccupations with noumena and phenomena—the essential and fleeting, that which is known to exist, but which escapes description, and that which can be described and is perceived through the senses. In addition, given the powerful metaphors associated with light, a medium that captures its ephemeral qualities through a mechanical apparatus, and further, fixes the perceived world through the actions of chemicals and on paper, gives photography (Sun-drawing or Heliography), enormous cultural significance.

This account will, by necessity, be brief, as it is meant more as a starting point for further research and exploration. In addition, it must be recognized that as the history of photography is not singular, neither is that of the museum, [1] or art or any movement associated with artistic practice such as modernism. The study of photography in any of its guises as art, as document, or as technology, therefore, requires the acknowledgment of the plurality of its other manifestations as well as an appreciation of the shifting social and political contexts that form and inform discourse at any particular point in time, including that of this review.

Throughout the nineteenth century, photography prompted diverse responses. In an era informed by the positivist spirit and colonial exploitation, the camera was an invaluable tool with which to record and categorize reality. In this respect, some commentators, such as Charles Baudelaire, denigrated the camera as soulless, cold, and mechanical. As a technology, photography participated in the "great

1 There are numerous publications on the history of museums, their cultural significance and how they affect interpretation of objects. See, for example Tony Bennett, *The Birth of the Museum: History, Theory, Politics* (London & New York: Routledge, 1995); Douglas Crimp, *On the Museum's Ruins* (Cambridge, Mass.: MIT Press, 1993); E. Hooper-Greenhill, *Museums and the Shaping of Knowledge* (London & New York: Routledge, 1992); Kenneth Hudson, *Museums of Influence* (Cambridge; New York : Cambridge University Press, 1987).

industrial madness" of the times that destroyed imaginative and creative pursuits. [2] Others, such as Oliver Wendell Holmes, were more enthusiastic. Holmes believed that photographs themselves would replace the objects photographed. In addition, the images could be gathered in comprehensive collections to the end of placing knowledge of the world at one's finger tips. [3] Yet other commentators recognized the social usefulness of the medium. Lady Eastlake stated that photography brought together "men of the most diverse lives, habits, and stations" [4]; the medium was a "new form of communication between man and man" [5] and useful in its transcription of reality. Marcus Aurelius Root also deemed photography beneficial as it provided "likenesses" of those held dear, but who, for whatever circumstances, were not present in one's daily life. [6]

2 Charles Baudelaire, "The Modern Public and Photography," in *Classic Essays on Photography*, Alan Trachtenberg, ed. (New Haven, Conn.: Leete's Island Books): 83-90.

3 Oliver Wendell Holmes, "The Stereoscope and the Stereograph," in Classic Essays, pp. 71-82. In this article, Holmes is speaking specifically of the stereograph. For an analysis of Holmes' ideas see Alan Sekula's essay "The Traffic in Photographs," in *Photography Against the Grain: Essays and Photo Works 1973-1983* (Halifax: Nova Scotia College of Art and Design, 1984):77-101.

4 Lady Elizabeth Eastlake, "Photography," in *Classic Essays*, p. 41.

5 Ibid., p. 65.

6 Marcus Aurelius Root, "The Camera and the Pencil," in *Photography in Print: Writings from 1816 to the Present*, Vicki Goldberg, ed. (Albuquerque: University of New Mexico Press, 1988): 148-151.

The century's debates concerning photography's artistry, however, were more contentious. Eastlake made several observations that pertain to the period's understanding of art and its relation to photography. Eastlake distinguished between art and Art. She understood photography more in terms of the former as it was "unerring," the "sworn witness of everything presented to her view." However, as she commented: "Correctness of drawing, truth of detail, and absence of convention, the best artistic characteristics of photography, are qualities of no common kind, but the student who issues from the academy with these in his grasp stands, nevertheless, but on the threshold of art." In her estimation, the medium did not allow for choice, or the "power of selection and rejection...the marriage of [the artist's] own mind with the object before him"[7]; in other words, that which the camera did so well, recording reality, demonstrated exactly what the medium was not—Art.

Other early practitioners, such as Henry Fox Talbot, understood photography in much the same manner. Photographs were "impressed by Nature's hand," and thus represented an exact inscription of its "immutable" laws.[8] In this respect, Talbot called his treatise on photography *The Pencil of Nature*; the camera transcribed nature, it was a "copyist." As for the expressive capacities of photography, Talbot was less than enthusiastic. In his treatise, he simply presented an image of a broom propped up in

7 Lady Elizabeth Eastlake, "Photography," in *Classic Essays*, p. 66.
8 Henry Fox Talbot, *The Pencil of Nature*, with a new introduction by Beaumont Newhall (New York: Da Capo Press, 1969): n.p.

front of an open door and declared that any artistry the work displayed was by association with the Dutch school of art that took ordinary objects as its subject matter to "awaken a train of thoughts and feelings, and picturesque images."[9]
The photographic journals of the time reveal how ideas of art and photography did not develop in exclusion, but were informed by the discourse and beliefs of a variety of disciplines. Journals ascribed both to ideas of progress and evolution in terms of technology (and thus the industrial, scientific and commercial uses of photography), as well as advising photographers on the artistry of the medium. However, the multiple capacities of photography were not overtly acknowledged and attempts to express the medium's plurality took shape within the period's cultural and conceptual parameters. For example, C. Jabez Hughes described three categories of photography: Mechanical, Art, and High-Art. The first of these was a "simple representation of the objects to which the camera was pointed." The second required more imagination as it embraced "all pictures where the artist, not content with taking things as may naturally occur, determines to infuse his mind into them by arranging, modifying, or otherwise disposing them, so that they may appear in a more appropriate or beautiful manner that they would have been without such interference." These intercessions include cropping, length of exposure, choice of enhancing materials, etc. The last category was the most difficult as it included works that "aim at a higher purpose than the majority of art-

9 Ibid., n.p.

photographs, and whose aim is not merely to amuse, but to instruct, purify, and ennoble."[10] In terms of this last category, Jabez Hughes' beliefs represented a leap of faith as most discounted photography's capacities to express such lofty ideals.[11]

Yet the idea that the photograph could depict a more elevated state of existence continued to have appeal. In order to consolidate these ideas of photography, and imbue a sense of solidarity among practitioners, photographers formed clubs for both the purpose of exchanging information and displaying works. In addition, the structure, hierarchy and semi-official status of clubs supported members in their belief of photography's "serious" intent.[12] Such efforts gained even greater urgency with the appearance of the hand-held camera, launched by George Eastman of Rochester, New York in July 1888. As now anyone could take a picture, it was necessary

10 C. Jabez Hughes, "On Art Photography," in *Photography Essays and Images: Illustrated Readings in the History of Photography*, Beaumont Newhall, ed. (New York: The Museum of Modern Art, 1980): 115.

11 However, to be considered Art, it was absolutely necessary that the medium assume this role To this end some, such as Oscar Rejlander, presented works such as "The Two Ways of Life" to demonstrate the ability of photography to "ennoble and instruct," although the work was controversial at the time. Some praised the message the work conveyed, youth choosing a life of either virtue or immorality. Others condemned the work for its blatant representation of unrighteous behavior. In addition, when it was discovered how Rejlander created the work, through an assembly of negatives, critics condemned it as "a thing of shreds and patches." See Henry Peach Robinson, "Oscar Gustav Rejlander," in *Photography: Essays and Images*, pp. 105-106.

to define the art of the medium more rigorously. Henry Peach Robinson, among others, established the Linked Ring Brotherhood as a means to promote photography as art both in Britain and internationally. [13] Pictorialist photographers, armed with gum bichromate and platinum emulsions produced works they deemed worthy to challenge the highest of the arts, painting, the very medium on which both the appearance and subject matter of their works was based. [14] However, photographers such as Berenice Abbott had little patience with the Pictorialists and their fuzzy depictions of the world that harkened back to old schools of painting. [15] Abbott advocated the

12 For more on the relation between photography as high art and the institutional makeup of camera clubs see Ulrich Keller, "The Myth of Art Photography: A Sociological Analysis," and "The Myth of Art Photography: An Iconographical Analysis," in the *History of Photography*, vol. 8, no. 4 (Oct.-Dec. 1984): 249-275; vol. 9, no. 1 (Jan.-Mar. 1985): 1-39, respectively.

13 In addition, the Linked Ring was a secessionist group, formed in response to the Photographic Society of Great Britain that emphasized only an empirical use of the medium. For more on this see Margaret Harker, *The Linked Ring: The Secessionist Movement in Photography in Britain*, 1892-1910 (London: Heineman Pub., 1979).

14 In light of the most recent art, such as Impressionism, Post-Impressionism, Fauvism, etc., the naturalist styles of painting being imitated by photographers were somewhat passé.

15 Abbott targets Henry Peach Robinson in particular for bringing the "terrible plague" of pictorialism to America: "Greatest disaster of all, he wrote a book in 1869 entitled *Pictorial Photography*. His system was to flatter everything."[Berenice Abbott, "Photography at the Crossroads, in *Classic Essays*, p. 181.]

"straight" school of photography, or a new, modern, and sharply focused vision of world. Laszlo Maholy-Nagy went even further and argued that the camera, in its objectivity, would "abolish that pictorial and imaginative associative pattern which has remained unsuperceded for centuries, and which has been stamped upon our vison by great individual painters." In this modernist vision of the machine aesthetic, photography "cleansed" history; the medium was to be celebrated as it would provide humanity with a new way of seeing.

This alignment of photography with ideas of progress and the modern was extended by Paul Strand to ideas of the nation. In the June 1917 edition of *Camera Work*, Strand proposed that an indigenous, American photographic practice existed, one formed and shaped by qualities "inherent" to the American spirit. For this he praised Alfred Stieglitz and his publication *Camera Work* for allowing "America [to be] expressed in terms of America without the outside influence of Paris art-schools or their dilute offspring...."[16] For Strand, photography had spontaneously developed in America as a result of "a small group of men and women [who] worked with honest and sincere purpose, some instinctively and few consciously, but without any background of photographic or graphic formulae, much less any cut and dried ideas of what is Art and what isn't; this innocence was their real strength. Everything they wanted to say had to be worked our by their own experiments; it was born of actual living."[17]

16 Paul Strand, "Photography," in *Photography: Essays and Images*, p. 220.
17 Ibid.

Strand placed photography outside history; its origins were spontaneous, its practitioners untutored, and its cultural inheritance denied.[18] However, even at the time of Strand's article, Stieglitz had already been instrumental in securing photography a place in one of its most powerful cultural contexts, the art museum. In his New York gallery 291, Stieglitz created a direct connection between art and photography with shows that included the works of Photo-Secessionists as well as the paintings and sculptures of Picasso, Rodin, and Matisse. He tirelessly promoted high art photography, at first through photography clubs, and later through his publications *Camera Notes* and *Camera Work*.[19] His efforts were slowly rewarded. In 1910, twelve works of the Photo-Secessionists were bought by the Albright Art Gallery in Buffalo[20] and in 1924, Stieglitz donated works to the Boston Museum of Fine Arts. Four years later,

18 Derrick Price and Liz Wells, "Thinking About Photography: Debates Historically and Now," in *Photography: a Critical Introduction*, edited by Liz Wells (London & New York: Routledge, 1997):27.
19 Alan Trachtenberg, "Pictorialist Photography, Alfred Stieglitz (1864-1946) and *Camera Work*," in *Classic Essays*, pp. 115-116. For more on American Pictorialism see Sara Greenough, "'Of Charming Glens, Graceful Glades, and Frowning Cliffs': The Economic Incentives, Social Inducements and Aesthetic Issues of American Pictorial Photography, 1880-1902," in *Photography in Nineteenth-Century*, Martha Sandweiss, ed. (New York: Harry N. Abrams, Inc. Pub. 1991): 258- 281.
20 See "The Photo-Secession at Buffalo: A Portfolio of Photographs Purchased by the Albright Gallery in 1910," in *Photography: Essays and Images*, p. 189.

the Metropolitan Museum of Fine Art in New York also received a gift of Stieglitz photographs. Other museums would soon follow suit. In 1930, the newly formed Museum of Modern Art in New York began to purchase photographs, and in1940 it created a Department of Photography. George Eastman House was established in 1949 as a photography museum. In addition, with the death of Stieglitz in 1946, the Philadelphia Museum of Art, the Art Institute of Chicago and the National Gallery of Art in Washington all received bequests of photography from the Stieglitz estate.

Although Stieglitz promoted high art photography through his gallery and publications, there still remained a lack of institutional recognition that would allow for both the collection of works, and their display within a larger aesthetic context. Most writers, in this respect, credit the Museum of Modern Art and its seminal exhibition *Photography, 1839-1937*, assembled by Beaumont Newall.[21] The genesis of the exhibition is usually understood to be a product of Alfred Barr's "genius" in recognizing the medium's inherent artistic qualities.[22] In the mid 1930s, Barr charged Newhall, then the Museum's librarian, with assembling a show on photography.[23]

21 See Douglas Crimp who in his book *On the Museum's Ruins* argues that it was both the Museum of Modern Art and the New York Public Library that decontextualized photography, and thus reduced its signifiying capacities.

22 Barr's interest in photography may have derived from European exhibitions, especially those developed through the Bauhaus. Another important photography exhibit was *Film und Foto*, assembled by Deutscher Werkbund in1929. For more on this see Mary Anne Staniszewski, *Power of Display: A History of Exhibition Installations*

With incredible confidence, Newhall, whose background was in art history, decided that he would do an historic survey based on stylistic analysis. [24] However, in spite of this initial idea, his catalogue *Photography 1839-1937*, gives little in terms of such an approach. [25]

at the Museum of Modern Art (Cambridge, Mass. : MIT Press, 1998): 44-55. For a more general history of the MoMA, see *The Museum of Modern Art: The History and the Collection,* introduction by Sam Hunter (New York: H.N. Abrams in association with the MoMA, 1993).

23 In Newhall's account of the event, the introduction of photography into the MoMA appears to have been more a product of collegial spirit: "Alfred Barr stopped me in a corridor and casually asked me, 'Would you like to put together a photographic exhibition? The trustees have approved it and we have a grant of five thousand dollars to cover expenses.' 'I sure would!' I answered. 'What kind of show do you want?' 'It's not what I want,' he replied. 'What would you like to do?'" [Beaumont Newhall, *Focus: Memoirs of a Life in Photography* (Boston: Little, Brown and Co., Inc., 1993): 43.]

24 As other writers have noted, Newhall studied at Harvard University whose courses in art history were developed by the connoisseur Bernard Berenson. In addition, Newhall took a museum course taught by Paul Sachs, himself a formalist connoisseur and assistant director of the Fogg Museum. [See Glenn Willumson "The Getty Research Institute: Materials for a New Photo-History," in *History of Photography*, Vol. 22, No. 1 (Spring 1991): 31.] Newhall recounts that another major influence was Fiske Kimball, director of the Philadelphia Museum. It was Kimball who introduced Newhall to the writings of Heinrich Wölfflin, Wilhelm Worringer, and Alois Riegel. Although such writers were disparaged at Harvard as being too spiritual, Newhall states that they always remained an inspiration and he hoped to reflect what he learned from them in his writing. [Beaumont Newhall, Focus, p. 39.]

Newhall lists the American and European collections from which he compiled his exhibition. Many now well-known photographers were approached such as Berenice Abbott, Ansel Adams, Walker Evans, Andre Kertesz, and Laszlo Maholy-Nagy, to name a few. In his catalogue Newhall recounts photography's history largely in terms of technical developments. There are chapters on daguerreotypes, calotypes, Bayard's paper positives, the collodion (wet plate) process, dry plate photography, colour photography, stereoscopic photography, and scientific photography. Outside these categorizations of the medium, sections such as contemporary photography, press photography and moving pictures, discuss the medium more in terms of description.

One is hard pressed to find in Newhall's writings the rarified vocabulary of modernist aesthetics.[26] Instead Newhall appears more as an affable raconteur, one who dutifully supplies a history of persons and events; photography and photographers are never taken up into larger metaphysical schemes. For example in a later article "Photography as Art in America" (which appeared in the Spring

25 See Mary Warner Marien's article "What Shall We Tell the Children? Photography and Its Text (Books)," in *Iluminations: Women Writing on Photography from the 1850s to the Present*, edited by Liz Heron & Val Williams (London & New York: I.B. Tauris, Pub., 1996): 207-222.

26 Such a stance can also be found in an earlier piece of writing, "Photography and the Artist." In this article, Newhall traces the presence and use of photography in the arts, but does not directly link photography and aesthetics. ["Photography and the Artist," *Parnassus*, vol. 6, no. 5 (Oct. 1934): 24-25; 28-29.]

1956 edition of *Perspectives USA*), the meaning of the word "art" is never qualified, but assumed. [27] Newhall traces a history of those who have professed to use the medium artistically, such as Peter Henry Emerson, Alfred Stieglitz, Edward Steichen, Edward Weston, etc., but he never really credits the medium as inherently possessing aesthetic qualities. Rather, he argues the opposite; the photograph is understood more from the point of view of reportage as it presents a clear and detailed vision of the world. For Newhall, aesthetics is useful as it "animates" a picture: "The innate power of the camera to produce believable, convincing records was all-important, but even greater was the imagination of the cameraman to vivify the facts." [28] As for photography's greater aesthetic capacities, Newhall, nearly a decade after his exhibition can only tentatively state at the end of the article that: "We are just beginning to learn [photography's] aesthetic potentials." [29]

27 Throughout the article, Newhall constantly aligns photography with nationalism; contributions to photography by those of other nationalities are acknowledged, but it is in America that their efforts gain fruition.

28 Beaumont Newhall, "Photography as Art in America," in *Perspectives USA* (Spring 1956):130.

29 Ibid., p. 133. See also Newhall's review of on Helmuth Bossert and Heinrich Guttman's book on photography where he states that the aesthetic of the medium lies in "the ability of the camera to capture the utmost possible detail of the natural world in its chief characteristic, and should be fully realized." [Beaumont Newhall, "Aus der Frühzeit der Photographie, 1840-70," in the *American Magazine of Art*, Vol. XXV, no. 2, p. 130-131.]

Newhall promotes photography's capacity to render a literal depiction of reality. The advancement of photography in this respect was also explored by Clement Greenberg. For Greenberg, photography excelled in its "transparency": "the art in photography is literary art before it is anything else...." The photograph attains an artistic status when "it calls the least attention to itself and lets the almost 'practical' meaning of the subject come through."[30] In addition, photographs became masterpieces by "transcending the documentary and conveying something that affects one more than mere knowledge ever could."[31] One, therefore, did not push an idea too much such as seen in the works of Henri Cartier-Bresson. In Greenberg's estimation, Cartier-Bresson's works were too stiff, contrived, frozen and "arty." For Greenberg, the art in photography was a product of delicately balanced conditions. The purely descriptive photograph was a "threat" to photographic art as such images did not convey the idea of the transcendent. Works which were "purely formal and abstract" did not express the medium's transparency.

30 Clement Greenberg, "Four Photographers, A Reprinted Review," in *History of Photography*, Vol 15, no. 2 (Summer 1991): 131.

31 Ibid. See also Greenberg's essay on Edward Weston. For Greenberg, painting had to rid itself of subject matter and become abstract. However, photography "is the only art that can still afford to be naturalistic and that, in fact, achieves its maximum effect through naturalism." To achieve the value of art, Greenberg pronounced "let photography be 'literary'." [Clement Greenberg, "The Camera's Glass Eye: Review of an Exhibition of Edward Weston," in Clement Greenberg: The Collected Essays and Criticism, Vol. 4, John O'Brian, ed. (Chicago and London: University of Chicago Press, 1993): 61.

Greenberg thus championed the works of Eugène Atget. Atget was
"humble" in his intentions: "He was not after beautiful views; he was
out to capture the identity of his subjects...." [32] In addition, Atget presented a more human world through "the signs and traces of the human
presence than from that presence itself." [33] For Greenberg, the world
became more immediately experienced through "distance." This allowed
the photographer to vivify the world (or "animate inanimate surface")
and thus create an art in photography. [34]
Newhall and Greenberg promote a very similar view of the art of photography, and the role of the photographer in terms of creative process.
There is detachment and distance; both the photographer and camera operate as impersonal devices animated by the creative spirit. The
photograph reveals how the union of aesthetics and technology
gives the world structure–aesthetics through form, line and tone,
and technology through optics, and the actions of light on chemicals.
Although Greenberg attempts to accommodate the technological
basis of photography within the tenets of high modernism, one senses

32 Ibid.

33 Ibid.

34 Ibid. See also Mike Weaver's article on Greenberg in the same issue. Weaver
argues that Greenberg and Walker Evans shared the same idea of the transcendent. The "great" photographer was one who experienced the world in a
heightened and impersonal way. As such, art in photography was achieved when
the photograph appeared spontaneous and not contrived, as if there were no
interceding agent. [Mike Weaver, "Clement Greenberg and Walker Evans, Transparency and Transcendence," in *History of Photography*, Vol. 15, no. 2 (Summer 1991): 128-130.]

that the medium sits uneasily in this scheme. As first seen in the writings of Lady Eastlake, there is a recurring anxiety that art cannot be produced through a mechanical device. Greenberg argued for immutable laws, ones that placed both the photograph and photographer outside specific historic and social contexts. For Greenberg, the more the object became isolated from reality, the more it was esteemed as a master work of art. Another commentator, John Szarkowski, also placed both photography and the photographer outside history; there was reality or "where [the] picture starts" but the photographer's "sense of craft or structure (where [the] picture is completed) are anonymous and untraceable gifts from photography itself."[35] In such a scheme, the photograph and photographer are isolated in a self-fulfilling, self-contained world. As the qualities of a photograph are undefined, a critical vocabulary for the medium would be difficult, if not impossible, to articulate.[36]

The intertwining of histories, that of art and photography, has resulted in a curious hybrid formed as a result of what Alan Sekula once termed the binary folklore of the medium.[37] At one end is

35 Ibid. In his book *The Photographer's Eye* John Szarkowski attempted to qualify the medium in terms of essential characteristics, ones that would define the medium as a thing in itself with its own history and properties. He argued, as did Strand, that photography "like and organism...was born whole." The medium appeared spontaneously, developing in terms of its own inner laws that are as yet still not understood. [John Szarkowski, *The Photographer's Eye*, (New York: MoMA, 1966): n.p.]

photography's symbolist or expressive capacities; in this scheme the world can be arranged within the camera's frame to express certain well established Western pictorial conventions. The type of subject matter chosen can also have iconographical significance. [38] At the opposite end is the realist, so-called documentary capacity of photography, or its ability to be used as reportage, or in granting evidence of events. Within the arguments of postmodernism, the symbolist and realist aspects of photography obtain their signification within larger cultural contexts. In other words, the photograph in itself cannot contain any essentialist message as its significance is dependant on who is viewing the image, where it is being seen, when and for what purposes-a set of conditions that allows for the generation of multiple meanings.

36 In *Photography Until Now*, Szarkowski completely dodges the issue of aesthetics "to sketch out a history of photographic pictures, organized according to patterns of technological change." For Szarkowski, photography is elusive, it is constantly changing, and as such, the "art" of the medium is seen in those works that embody "the clearest, most eloquent expression of photography's historic and continuing search for a renewed and vital identity." [John Szarkowski, *Photography Until Now* (New York: MoMA, 1989): 9.] One could argue that this view is progressivist in the sense that there is the idea that both technology and art will at some future point coincide, each finding perfect expression through the other.
37 Alan Sekula, "On the Invention of Photographic Meaning," in *Thinking Photography*, Victor Burgin, ed. (London: Macmillan, 1982): 108.
38 One has only to think of "Migrant Mother" (1936) by Dorthea Lange, or Lewis Hine's "A Madonna of the Tenements" (1911).

Within the histories of photography, there have been many who have argued for the medium's fine art status. There has been a persistent desire to temper the mechanics of the photographic apparatus with a creative spirit, and humanize through technology the effects of technology. The debates concerning the medium's artistry have been varied and sometimes self-contradictory, a challenge to those who defend one idea of the medium over others. However, it is the diversity of these ideas and the variety of stances taken that indicate the cultural richness of the photography.

This essay has addressed only a few of the factors that have formed ideas of the medium's aesthetic capacities. The alignment of photography as art with consumer culture, the role of cultural institutions such as art museums, archives, universities and colleges, the significance of the collector, the publishing industry, biennials and issues surrounding private and state patronage are other factors to be considered. Photography can only be understood within a complex of conditions, themselves mutable and responsive to greater social, economic, and political concerns. Its art lies in its ability to depict this diversity– not isolate itself from such considerations.

Andrea Kunard, is an essayist and curator at the Canadian Photography Museum in Ottawa.

RECYCLING OF REALITY: SEARCHING FOR A HISTORICAL INFRA-STRUCTURE
FROM PARADOX TO PAROXYSM

Johann Swinnen

Beaumont Newhall has provided with the dominant interpretative pattern for the history of photography, in which most of museums collections are based. Basically it is the history of a technology that leads towards different ways of visual representation, with an emphasise in authors and aesthetic movements. What is this approach missing?

One had to wait one and a half centuries before photography could arouse sincere interest in historians. This does not mean that during all this time – which, in the perspective of history, can still be considered rather short – no contemplation's or publications took place. However, they lacked a solid methodological basis and the ambition to provide sufficient theoretical explanation.

It was not until 1989, exactly 150 years after the invention of the medium of photography that, in addition to the many albums presenting themselves as "the world history" of photography, excellent monographs emerged, resulting from patient research in often difficult circumstances. Remarkable essays, studying a development in time and revealing little known or concealed facts, schools or periods frequently accompany them. In addition, an important group of "young photographers" has tackled the history of photographic expression, in an attempt to determine the specificity of their medium and how it conflicts with other forms of expression. In so doing, they want to retrieve a strict photographic tradition before adding their own photo production to this tradition.

The history of photographic representation, however, is a controversial field. Therefore, we see ourselves confronted with a change regarding the conditions of traditional historical research. Since photography shapes time, turns it around, interrupts life to perpetuate the moment, and thus conceives rules which determine the approach to its past, its history is only possible as a function of the future perspectives the medium holds for itself. Now in 2000 that photography – on very weak ground theoretically, but clearly recognised as a contemporary medium – searches for its rightful stature, it is even more important that history informs us, albeit about the errors, the ambiguities, the compromises of a form of expression which is normally praised to the rafters by those who feel called to discuss it.

Benjamin stated that we should rethink photography and history altogether, because what transforms an event in an historical event is it's technical reproducibility (its photographic recording). The language of photography articulates history and at the same time history gives meaning to photography. In regard to this paradox, how to approach a history of photography?
So, more than ever, the history of photography in the year 2000 is ambiguous. It shows something, a fragment of reality framed by the camera or in the darkroom which, considering the objectivity of the process, can lay significant claim to factual knowledge. Each one also asks a question: what is the reality-value of an image? And how is the objective de-objectified by the subjectivity of the maker and the viewer, augmented by the contextual influences on both. This ambiguity has been called the 'paradox of photography'. It is Barthes in particular who opposes the *'doxa'*. The *'doxa'* is the view that derives its strength from power in the broadest sense of the word:

public opinion, the view of the silent majority, the narrow-minded view, everything that is so-called 'natural', the violence of prejudice, that which one maintains *is* so because it *is* so. The metaphorical sense of the word *'para'* in Greek is 'against'. *'Para tein doxan'* means 'against expectations'. This last word at the same time makes the link with psychology, which assumes that our perception is determined by expectation. The paradox starts us thinking, in order to adjust our expectation to the actual situation. If not we are 'dogmatic', a word with the same stem as *'doxa'*, which refers to the unwillingness to change one's opinion. Barthes argues for paradoxical thinking. Photography states this paradoxically most acutely. Every photo is a *doxa*: it is reality the way it is, in many cases even with demonstrative force. Or as John Berger put it*: 'Less than thirty years after its invention as an amusing device for the elite, photos were being used for police archives, war reporting, military reconnaissance, pornography, encyclopaedic documentation, family albums, postcards, anthropological reports, sentimental moral lessons, aggressive investigation (erroneously called 'candid camera'), aesthetic effects, news services and official portraits.*

How to present a 'political correct' history of photography? How the social minorities could be introduced, how was the Third World contributed…?'
Two approaches seem possible. One is through clearly demarcated investigations into photographers, studios, groups and periods, which are hardly or only superficially known. On the other hand, African, Oriental, and South American photography – to mention what

presently has not yet been studied – is an important area to be investigated. This historiography considered as an increase of knowledge and awareness of its limitations could mean progress in the theory of photography, particularly if it would parallel more ambitious projects such as a transversal and diachronic historical analysis relating elements which now tend to disappear in the senseless litany of the chronology of photography. Provided these projects treat their subject with the necessary critical reserve, they will be very important for the photography of the future.

What should be more relevant, a history of artists or a history of images?

However, every photo is a paradox: it is a picture of reality, or in other words it is a way of seeing. And that should not be taken too simply, as no more than a relativization by accentuating the fact that it is a 'way' of looking, coupled with the conviction that it actually is reality. Its 'image-dom' implies that it is not reality, that it is a way of representation, that in our pan-photographic culture we have learnt that this reality as such cannot say anything with any certainty that we do not know from other sources of information, such as direct observation or verbal explanation. Without these extra-photographic data, photography remains in utter silence. Is the photo a testimony of war or a still from a war film? But it is precisely this questioning unknowing that opens up a path, that of the interpretation which can only occur at the level of photographic singularity, where the reality to which is being referred is unimportant or can only be seen as 'material' in addition to the other specific characteristics. This sounds disrespectful when it concerns people, but in a photo it is of no importance who this working-class person is or who that down-and-outer is and which part of the Third World he comes from, or who that self-satisfied middle-class citizen may be. After all it is all about aspects of humankind itself. In this sense, as a non-showing (we do not know the reality) showing (we wonder interpretatively), photography is close to the unknowing knowing of philosophy.

Which are the main trends (cultural, ideological, political...) that have ruled the dominant historiographic models?

A conception of photography akin to Barthes can be found in the writings of Susan Sontag, who describes photography as a 'recycling of reality' and even as 'a devouring/predatory way of looking'
Her essay 'In Plato's cave' gives a detailed account of her approach to the problem at stake. Just like in the allegory of the cave, in which the people in chains mistake the shadows they can perceive for the truth, we are still stubbornly gaping at the shadows of this world and are deceived by their appearances. The origin of this problem lies within the fact that the deceiving shadow images of photography are a different type of shadow than a painting or another 'crafted' type of representation. Photography, which in the meantime has photographed (drawn up an inventory of) virtually everything paved the way for a new visual code. It decides upon what is to be photographed and what ought not to not be. This gives us the impression that we can register and store the entire world in our brain in the manner of a series of pictures. This series of pictures, which can be produced cheaply and easily, have in the meantime become objects in their

own right, by means of which we are in the position to annex and usurp the entire world.

Photographing things equals appropriating things. Because photography has become so intimately intertwined wit the compulsive idea that anything of importance ought to be photographed; the opposite also becomes true. Whatever has been photographed, is important. Susan Sontag concludes: 'The omnipresent camera leads to the convincing suggestion that time is made up out of interesting events, events which are worthwhile to be photographed.'

When an event is over and has receded in time, there still remains the photograph which will preserve it for eternity. The written word is much less capable to accomplish this. Writing automatically entails an interpretation and representations crafted by human hands suffer from the same shortcomings.

Photographs bear a close resemblance to a miniature reality that can be made by anybody. Despite the fact that the photograph is a two-dimensional object, can be blown up or miniaturised, translates colour in shades of grey, is being manipulated and touched up, we still insist on seeing it as a genuine unadulterated parcel of reality. Reality, deprived of the dimension of time, is granted the status of immortality. A supplementary advantage of photographs is that, in comparison with other representations, they lose but little of their original character in the process of reproduction. The formal resemblances between a photograph and its reproduction in a publication are striking indeed.

In her essay 'Melancholy objects', Susan Sontag elaborates upon Barthes' definition of photography as 'frottage', by advancing the theory that, precisely because of its very realism, photography is the most intrinsically surrealist of all artistic mediums: in fact, it is the only art that has been able to perform this most terrifying and age-old menace of a surrealist coup on modern sensibility.

The argument departs from the assumption that photographs are taking over the place of reality, because of the simplified and at the same time credible image which they produce of it. As such, Sontag's theory hardly pertains to the 'solarisations' and 'rayographies' by Man Ray, Moholy Nagy's photograms, the collages by George Hugnet and the assemblages and staged photography by pop artists and in contemporary photography. She goes so far as to label the discoveries of the eighties as 'marginal', and adopts a polemic stance with regard to the inclination of both photographs and critics to cluster in schools. According to her line of reasoning, and as opposed to the art of painting, there is only one type of photography and, as a whole, it is of an overall eclectic and global nature, operates by annexation and is closely connected with reality.

Are compatibles in photography a social history with an aesthetic history, a history of uses with a history of forms?`

It is obvious that there is a vacancy for semiotics in the field of philosophy, as a complement to aesthetics. In this respect, Umberto Eco provides us with a relevant illustration, borrowed from his own experience: '*I had written four books on aesthetics before I got interested in semiotics, but also after that, I always continued my research in the field of art.*' Aesthetics is not a neatly confined discipline, which could only be approached via a psychological or a metaphysical methodology: it is a much broader, more inclusive domain. Because of the fact that I am attracted by what cannot immediately be expressed by means of words, yet cannot stand that certain things remain undebatable –cannot be spoken about–, I use semiotics as a way of approaching certain problems and to elucidate some aspects thereof. Of course, an aesthetic experience cannot be grasped or quantified by means of semiotics, but the latter can be instrumental in explaining some of its characteristics. When I deal with the problem of colour, as was the case on the occasion of the lecture on Mondriaan, I start out by means of a categorisation in a first instance. But still, the fact remains that, beyond a certain point, our aesthetic experience of colour blows away all these categorisations. And yet, it is language that provides us with the possibility of conveying new, unknown colours as Joyce did.

In the above quotation, Willem Elias finds a formulation of the importance of the relationship between semiotics and aesthetics: *"On the one hand, it is a conflicting or contradictory one, since the former is usually approached in a quantitative manner, whereas the latter deals with impressions of a qualitative nature; on the other hand, a combination of both is experienced as an enrichment, in the sense that they both complement each other and fill the gaps between them."* And that is a truly engaging experience indeed.

Can contemporary photography be considered as an autonomous discipline or it would it be more useful to analyse its applications in other fields?

In the first place, contemporary photography is characterised by an approach to photography that actually does depart from reality, yet renders this reality from a very specific angle/perspective as a result of the photographic technique and design it employs. More in particular, the processes that are typical of the medium of photography such as, for instance, repetition, paradox and the gap between actual reality and its representation, are often recurred to. This contemporary, emphatically visually oriented photography is characterised by a certain degree of alienation from reality as the latter can be perceived and often stands out by its markedly illusory character.

Photography is able to create a duplicate world/reality that is of a more dramatic nature than the natural world. By imaging this reality in a fragmented manner, the photographer suggests that there is a need for an– other, a second reality which ought to be conquered by the photographer.

In the second place, one needs to point out that contemporary photography is quite ambiguous. It consists of showing a parcel of reality, framed by the camera or in the dark room, and -considering the objective nature of this procedure- is entitled to lay serious claims to thorough epistemological validity or genuine knowledge of reality. In addition to this, it is at the same time a calling into question of the reality value of a given image and of the manner in which the objective is being 'dis-objectified' by the subjectivity of both the creator and of the spectator, which, in turn, is enhanced by contextual influences on and conditioning of both of these. This very ambiguity has been called the paradox of photography. The art of photography presents this paradox in its most acute and incisive manner. Each and every photograph constitutes a doxa: it is reality as it is, quite often with conclusive argumentative evidence.

Could it be more philosophical ?

A photographer freezes reality in an image. That stasis opens the way to interpretation. The right moment has gone ('ça-a-été') and space has been demarcated two-dimensionally, possibly with the illusion of the third dimension, depth.

Through this framing the organisation of the image becomes the starting-point for a possible interpretation. There is a search for a correct framework. Knowledge of context is a prerequisite for the understanding of the image. This knowledge is not always provided verbally, since the photograph is an autonomous image. So that the viewer has to guess the correct category to be able to classify the image. With most images that is relatively easy, otherwise images would be constantly driving us crazy. We deal with photographs as we do with reality. But some images confuse us. And that is the case with these exceptional images by exceptional photographers. Within photography there is also a special 'category' of surprising images. This derives not from the fact that they are spectacular, but from the alienating stillness that they emanate.

Up to now I have restricted myself to a fairly abstract definition of the theme, but I can be more concrete. The easily classifiable images are the so-called normal images. The photographs I am concerned with here do not show an abnormal world, but the no-man's-land between normal and abnormal.

For instance, you might wonder about the limits of intimacy. Intimacy derives from 'intimus', the 'innermost', the superlative of 'inside', which in turn is an intensification of 'in'. But up to what point does that progression inwards remain intimate? As far as the ritual slaughter and devouring of the beloved? Or is that murder? How far does a party remain a party? Where and when does eroticism become pornography? Where, for instance, do the extremes of madness and genius meet? Some photographers have investigated these questions by photographing such borderline situations. These are images that themselves question the category to which they belong. They do so by going to extremes. In this way they move a fraction closer to the other category, but without actually moving into that other category. 'Where is the boundary?' is the cliché question asked in such circumstances. The fact is, that the boundary is not anchored in reality, but is rather a construct of our routine way of looking. How small or large can that fractional difference be? The word fraction is very appro- priate here, namely because of its definition as a 'quantity less than a whole', but that quantity may be large. In addition, the origin of the word 'fraction' is the Latin 'frangere', meaning 'break'. The boundary is a fault line in any case.

One could denote this phenomenon with the word 'paroxysm'. The Oxford English Dictionary gives the following meanings for paroxysm:

1. increase in the acuteness or severity of a disease;

2. violent access of action or emotion;

3. an open quarrel.

At first sight the term may not seem appropriate, but French theorists (cfr. Jean Baudrillard) occasionally use it as an image. They are always referring to the intensity of the borderline. Disease is infinite before the quantifiability of death. Intense rage or suffering know no bounds to their expression. A volcanic eruption may be a tourist attraction or the explosion of the earth itself. The exhibition is about extremes, about attempts to escape from a category in which one had pigeonholed oneself.

So in this case paroxysm refers to the questioning of the boundary between (mutually exclusive) pairs of concepts like incident and accident, animal and vermin, man and monster, calm and storm, plants and weeds, deed and misdeed, but also like love and hate, pleasure and pain, peace and war, science and myth, medicine and witchcraft, in short, all kinds of concepts that we can accommodate in the polarities of normal and abnormal. Contemporary photography explore the no-man's-land between the two extremes.

In your opinion, what's has been actually done, a true history of photography or just a sort of archaeology?
This is why a philosophy of the history of photography comes down to asking the classic questions: What are its characteristics? How can one interpret it? What is its value? How does it function and within which systems? How is meaning produced? All this makes a contribution to the fundamental *philosophical* question: what is photography?

Johann Swinnen is a historian and director of the HIFA in Antwerp.

THE INSTANT OF HISTORY
Vincent Lavoie

The ambition of this article is to elucidate the contribution that photography has made to the representation of the event, given that photography has played a major role in forging a new culture of the event that is inseparable from the development of technology and the idea of performance with regard to current events. The news, which means, in fact, shortening as much as possible the intervals between what happens, the representation of the event and its diffusion, appears at the very start of photography as the object of a quest. The immediacy of the event is exactly what photography seeks and that subsequent forms of media – live T.V., video surveillance in public areas, televised ceremonies and, more recently, the review of the major events of the 20th Century through the use of photographs – have exacerbated as the only criteria for validating historical representation.

The event of mediatisation

Photography introduces a relation to the event that is inseparable from the will to communicate it. As early as the 1840's, when daguerreotypes were being copied by hand to appear in the illustrated journals of the time, the mass diffusion of iconographies was already the order of the day. As the editor of a daily paper said at the time, nothing happens that is not immediately photographed and diffused to the general public [1]. However, the time that elapsed between

1 "A man can not ask a woman for a date nor may she turn him down – nor a boiler explode or a river break its banks - a gardener can not elope with an inheritress nor can a reverand make a slip, without a daguerreotype immediately rushing forth to expose it to the whole world". Cf. "Picture Pausings, No. II. Daguerreotypes", *Christian Watchman* 27, no. 20, 15 May 1846, p, 77 ;

the taking of the picture and its reproduction in the form of a drawing was rather long (one week to ten days) and this was a handicap in terms of the public's response to the event. Having to rely on drawings in order to ensure the public diffusion of the daguerreotype was another handicap of no small measure. From the 1850's onwards, photographs could be reproduced using lithography, but the process was expensive and therefore only used for limited editions and since picture and text could not yet be printed on the same page, the mass diffusion of the photograph was still not possible.

It was not until the 1860's and the appearance of the stereoscope, a device that had been developed to quantify and formalise the physiology of binocular vision, that a genuine market for the spectacle of the photograph was born. Long before the rise of the illustrated magazine in the 1920's, stereographs were being produced on an industrial scale in response to the new craving for the shock of the image. The stereoscope, in the same way as other devices such as the phenakistoscope, the thaumatrope and the zoetrope, was part of the " epistemological break " that founded a new concept of vision[2]. The advent in the 1820's of new social and discursive practices and the renewal of the status of the perceiving subject as well as the birth of a new cultural economy, are at the origin of this change. Designed initially for scientific observations, but quickly converted into forms of popular entertainment, these optical instruments played an active part the in rise of the culture of the spectacle.

If the realism of stereoscopic pictures partially explains their popularity, how they were viewed and diffused is mainly what helps us to understand their role in the development of a cultural vision of the masses. Their popularity depended first of all of the way they were observed. The massive production of stereographs incited and stimulated the compulsive consumption of images designed to feed the spectator's curiosity. Need it be said that pornographic pictures made up a large part of the stereoscopic market and that the spectacular illusionism of the pictures satisfied a purely ocular desire to possess. Viewing a large number of these images was part of the very logic of the process, meaning one visual surprise after another. It is in this sense that the content of the images is less important than the pleasure that is associated with the mass reception of a profusion of images. Thus, the stereoscopic industry founded a relation to visual mediatisation based on a repertoire of pictures that were constantly renewed by bands of photographers.

in Michael L. Carlebach, *The Origins of Photojournalism in America*, Washington, Smithsonian Institution Press, 1992, p. 2-3.

2 In Jonathan Crary, *Techniques of the Observer. On Vision an Modernity In the Nineteenth Century*, Cambridge ; Mass., MIT Press, 1990 and in particular the first chapter entitled "Modernity and the Observer" in which the author associates the appearance of these new instruments with the disappearance of a paradigm that served both as an explicative model of vision as well as the paragon for the morphogenesis of the photographic apparatus : the camera obscura. Crary goes on to dismantle this paradigm which is one that historians usually resort to to legitimise the place photography holds in the tradition of visual representation. Crary explains that the camera obscura, which is where a number of discursive practices converge (scientific, philosophical, cultural and social) and a paradigmatic model of the rational and empirical thought of the 17th and 18th Centuries, is not part of the modern history of vision.

The conditions in which the stereograph was viewed, and which in many ways prepared the way for the cinema, show quite clearly that this industry is one of the spectacle. As Rosalind Krauss points out, the stereograph, in the same way as the cinema, isolates the spectator from the outside world and introduces him to a place of darkness, a theatre of simulation, in which illusory representations are revealed. Stereographs, to which the author attributes a leading role in the proto-history of cinematographic simulation[3], produce not only the illusion of depth but also the impression of a '' dilation in time '' which the author attributes to '' the long and thorough exploration of every space '' that can be seen in the picture. This impression of optical displacement, also produced by the diorama, is the result of a series of accommodations that the stereograph exerces on the spectator's eye. The most effective pictures are those in which an element in the foreground obstructs the middle ground and forces the eye towards another obstructing element, and then to another, and so on. Rosalind Krauss notes this optical phenomenon in several topographical pictures taken by Timothy O'Sullivan in the 1860's. Indeed, several have a feature in the centre - a tree, a landscape etc. – around which the rest of the picture is composed. The spectacle is all the more convincing when the representation contains a host of details and even a certain degree of chaos.

3 "What has been called the *mechanism* of the cinematographic process had, then, a certain proto-history in the development of the stereograph, which evolved itself from another dark space, the diorama, where the spectator was isolated and offered a spectacular illusion of reality '' Rosalind Krauss, "Les espaces discursifs de la photographie", *in Le photographique. Pour une théorie des écarts*, Paris, Macula, 1990.

The photogenic catastrophe

The bourgeois interiors of the time, in which the overabundance of objects mitigated a horror of the void, were valued for this very reason, as were the representations of accidents or catastrophes which, being diametrically opposed to domestic peace, offered visual surprises of the chaotic. Hence, the derailing of a train or the ruins of a building after a fire attracted the photographers' attention due to the formal anarchy that is peculiar to this type of subject. Indeed, the public's predilection for pictures of catastrophes was the very backbone of the rising economy of the event[4]. More than a tragedy or a disaster, the derailing of a train or a city fire provided the occasion to mobilise a large number of actors in the communications industry – photographers, artists, reporters, editors, printers, retailers etc. – essential to the rise and development of the mass media.

The economic aspect alone does not explain the origins of the public's interest in this type of imagery, and particularly the photographers'. The tragedy was lucrative because it was photogenic, even `` picturesque '' as Elerslie Wallace said when describing pictures showing a railway accident. In an article published in 1893, he described the derailing of a locomotive as `` a picturesque mass of railway wreckage''[5]. The

4 ``Events such as railroad wrecks and the fires that plagued Americain cities in the latter half of the nineteenth century were considered by some members of the photographic fraternity to be more than tragedy or disaster. Stereographs of city fires sold well, and the tabloids could always counted on to run illustrations of the smokey ruins.'' Michael L. Carlebach, *op, cit.*, p. 151.

5 Elerslie Wallace, *American Annual of Photography, 1893*, p. 34-35 ; cité in *Id., Ibid.*, p. 151.

public's interest in this kind of event was not new. From the 1850's onwards daguerreotypes were being produced that showed similar catastrophes. However, having to resort to engraving to reproduce these pictures in the best-selling tabloids of the time, altered somewhat the ''picturesqueness'' of the scene. The illustrations copied from daguerreotypes rarely gave a true rendering of the original. The artists did not hesitate to change the general aspect of any scene that the photographer had captured too quickly or in a way that was not fitting. They compensated for any ''mistake'' by adding or removing certain details from the original representation. At least this is what

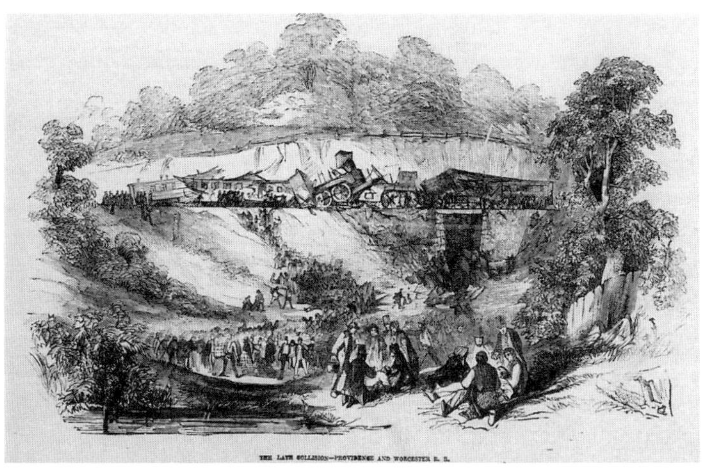

Illustration after a daguerreotype by L. Wright showing a derailing of a train on the Providence-Worcester line. Engraving on wood. *New York Illustrated News,* 27 August 1853.

can be seen in an illustration copied from a daguerreotype produced by L Wright, that was reproduced in the *New York Illustrated News* on August 27, 1853 and that showed the derailing of a train on the Providence-Worschester line. Whereas the original bears elements that are not very easy to make out or identify, such as the people who, due to the dramatic turn of events, are in a state of commotion and out of focus, or the debris of all sorts that can be confused with other elements in the landscape, the engraving, on the other hand, shows a well-ordered composition in which the people present are standing in lines or in clearly defined groups. The cause of the drama seems far removed and belittled by the landscape in the background. Most of the dramatic tension is concentrated on the wounded and dying in the foreground who are represented with all the traits of the traditional emotional vocabulary.

The actuality of the event

The use of the engraving and in particular the involvement of the artist's hand and eye, led to the removal of the signs and metonymies associated with any emergency – the blur, movement, truncated bodies, lack of focus or composition – as seen in the photographic image. In other words, communicating the event through the use of the graphic illustration meant sacrificing the edges – the panic (as much the people's as the photographer's), the disorder, the emptiness – that photography, as early as the 1850's, had included as the main attributes of immediacy. Often unwanted, sometimes too blunt but necessary nonetheless to the expression of the actuality of the event, such heterogeneous elements are what enabled photography to assert itself as the image-event. Due to the pictorial conventions governing them, the graphic arts reconstructed the event and had to emphasis the high point of the drama, the most representative episode of the event, the moral side of the tragedy, in order to ensure that the picture maintained its value as a demonstration and a lesson.

Instantaneous photography, which appeared in the 1880's, upset the criteria that gave the representation of the event its validity. However, this led to a profound transformation of the codes of historical illustration. The proof being that at the end of the 19th Century, the illustration had taken on the shape of the instantaneous photograph. As Michel Frizot says `` To feign a display of terror, any illustration, even of the most banal piece of news, expressed the same vision of time at a sudden stop, the same freezing of the moment, as the snapshot did[6]." Indeed, having to face competition from the photographic model and remain credible, the illustration, it appears, had to borrow a certain number of features that characterised photography. Thus, the illustration assimilated the features of the instantaneous photograph which, progressively, replaced the acme of the past. From the end of the 1870's, even though instantaneity had not yet overturned the practices in the field of the illustrated press, the historical illustration was already incorporating the main attributes of instantaneous photography. The action that the artists chose to illustrate maintained the prestigious rhetoric of the catastrophe but to it, they associated the credibility of the instantaneous.

6   Michel Frizot, "Faire face, faire signe. La photographie, sa part d'histoire", in *Face à l'histoire. L'artiste moderne devant l'événement historique 1933-1996*, Paris, Centre Georges Pompidou, 1996, p. 53.

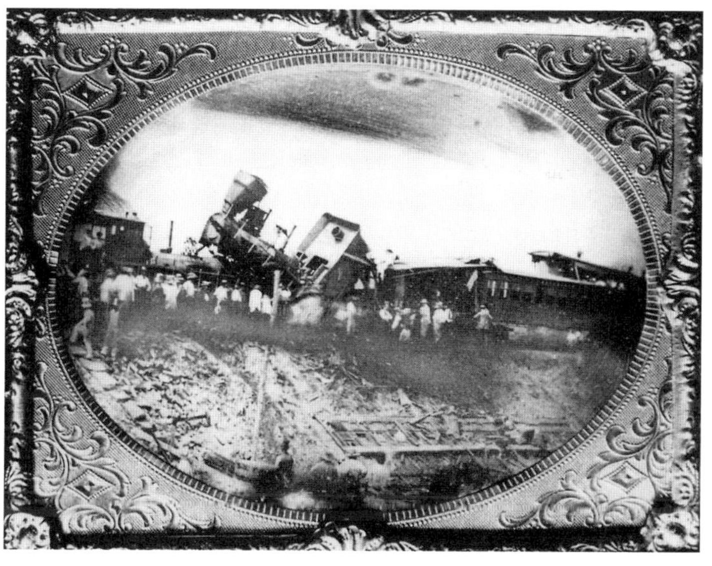

L. Wright, Derailing of a train on the Providence-Worcester line. Daguerreotype. International Museum of Photography at George Eastman House. 1853.

An engraving which illustrates the clash between the police and the railway workers during the strikes in 1877 is a good example of this. The picture shows the troops of the Union firing at the demonstrators. The illustration, that was reproduced in *Harper's Weekly*, evokes, of course, *The execution of the Emperor Maximilian of Mexico* by Edouard Manet and *The 3rd of May 1808: The Execution of the Defenders of Madrid* by Francesco Goya. To produce this image, the engraver doubtlessly drew from these references, which had become popular at the time as engravings indeed. More than merely borrowing from the iconography of these works, the cloud of smoke produced by the military weapons, which in Manet's work is intensified to such a degree as to crystallise the essence of most commentaries that underline the painting's modernity, belonged at this time to a set of references that are more photographic than pictorial. As a true metonymy for detonation, which in a photograph is a very particular exercise in style, the cloud is the emblematic expression of the instantaneous.

In their decisive work on the "discovery" of instantaneous photography, Denis Bernard and André Gunthert reveal how events such as explosions and fireworks were valued by the photographic fraternity, preoccupied as they were by the will to capture even the most fleeting of phenomena. The explosion was indeed a considerable challenge to the instantaneous photographer. The proof of this is the fact that any successful photograph i.e. one that captured the most emblematic moment of the event, was heralded as a triumph. The attraction exerted by the explosion was such that in the 1880's, beyond its empirical value, it became a curio. As a champion of the instantaneous photograph, Albert Londe, whose life and works are the object of Bernard and Gunthert's study, describes in the following terms the spectacle produced by the explosion of dynamite in the stone quarry in Argenteuil, an explosion that afforded him two pictures, "There was a heavy silence in the quarry: only a few wisps of smoke indicated that the operation had begun. Suddenly there was the sound of an explosion and there were stones flying all around us. Other explosions followed and the pillars of stone fell one after the other[7]." At a similar explosion in a gypsum quarry in Volambert, the head of the scientific magazine *Nature* compared the hoard of photographers to a firing squad : "Just as the explosion was about to go off, about thirty cameras took aim and all fired at the same time, like a bunch of musketeers[8]." The fire of the musketeers' smoke is exactly what the engraving by Bendann shows: a cloud that stands for one of the most typical features of instantaneous photography. Even if the moment that the artist cares to show is extremely brief – the space of a detonation – it is simply because from here on, history is an expression of the instantaneous. Because what the picture in *Harper's Weekly* shows is, of course, a chapter in American social history but it is above all the reduction of this very history to a single, emblematic moment in time.

Beyond the shock of actuality

The principal that turns the instantaneous representation of the event into a moment of history, was introduced by photography, there can be no doubt about it. The recent editorials have reminded us

7   Albert Londe, "Les carrières à plâtre d'Argenteuil. Leur mode d'exploitation", *La Nature*, n. 621, t. 2, 21 November 1885, p, 395-398 ; Denis Bernard and André Gunthert, *L'instant rêvé. Albert Londe*, Nîmes/Laval, Editions Jacqueline Chambon/Editions Trois, 1993, p. 225.
8   Gaston Tissandier, "Société d'excursions des amateurs photographes", *La Nature*, n. 747, t. 2, 24 September 1887, p. 264 ; Denis Bernard and André Gunthert, *op. cit.*, p. 224.

of this principal and underlined the considerable contribution that the photography of the press has made in building a collective memory. References are made to many a publication containing the most famous pictures of the 20 th Century but these have only been appeared over the past few years[9]. Whether it is the shot that shows the heroic death of the republican soldier during the Spanish Civil War or the picture of a young Vietnamese girl being burned by napalm, or else the German soldier crossing over to the West or the burning to death of the Buddhist monk, the principal is always the same: the photograph of the event crystallises the most significant episodes of history. So that sometimes a single picture – and there are many of them – is enough to sum up a certain period of time. The most emblematic are often those that concentrate into a single, dramatic moment the difficulty of the whole situation at that time in history.

It is certainly in reaction to the impact produced by the shock of the news, and in an attempt to renew the links with the experience of the event, that certain authors, even if they have to resort to pictures from the press have wanted " *to get back to the picture* ", as Annick Cojean said in her work published in 1997 [10]. As an experienced reporter for the newspaper *Le Monde* the author, in the introduction

9 One of the most significant examples of the publications dealing with the important photographic documents of the century is the work by Marie-Monique Robin, *Les Cent Photos du siècle*, Paris, Éditions du Chêne, 1999.
10 Annick Cojean, *Retour sur images*, Paris, Grasset/Le Monde, 1997. This is a collection of thriteen articles that appeared in the summer of 1997 in the daily newspaper *Le Monde*.
11 op. cit., p. 10.

to her work, says she wanted to "put an end to fantasy, to get as close as possible to the truth of the moment fixed by the camera. To stop imagining"[11]. The author sought this truth by going to meet the people who had been immortalised by the moment. However, the conditions in which the pictures were taken, it appeared, were less important than the upheaval they caused in the personal lives of those who were photographed. " Getting back to the picture " as proposed by the author, implies going further than merely perceiving the famous current event depicted in the photograph. Indeed, what catches the attention are the circumstances that followed the event that was photographed – or perhaps we should talk about the photographic event if we bear in mind the repercussions that its wide-spread diffusion had. More than an expression of a current event, the picture is in most cases, the basis of a story that the interview brings to light. If, as privileged witnesses to the event, the interviewees recall the context in which the photograph was taken, they do so in order to express how much the " photographic event " had a bearing on their own individual " history ".

One of the most convincing examples of how long-lasting a photograph's actuality can be in an individual's life is certainly that of *Marianne* in May 1968. The photo was taken by Jean-Pierre Rey in the Latin Quarter of Paris. Sitting on the shoulders of a man in the middle of crowd of demonstrators, a young lady was waving a Vietnamese flag. The solemn pose, the serious face, the crowd she is above and the flag were enough for the picture to be compared to the painting *Liberty leading the people* by Delacroix. The reference to his *Marianne*, in addition to posing the problem of the origins of what is a

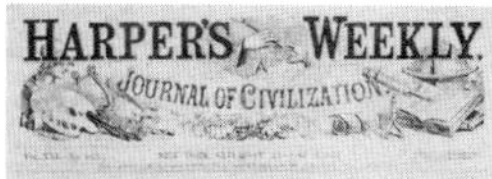

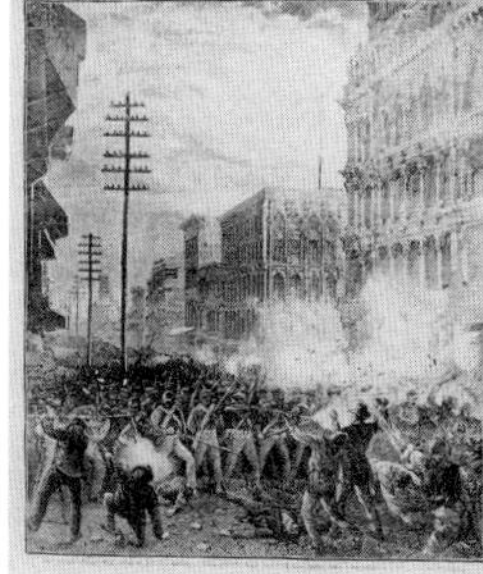

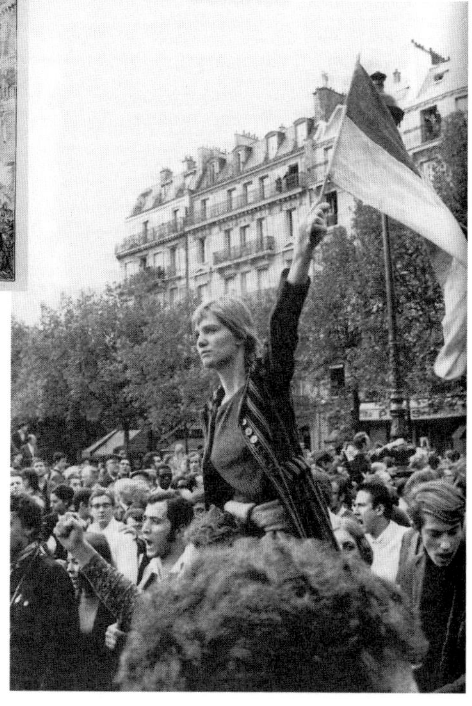

Illustration after a photograph by David Bendann showing American troups shooting at railway workers on strike in Baltimore, Maryland. Engraving on wood. *Harper's Weekly*, 11 August 1877.

Jean-Pierre Rey/Rapho, Paris, Quartier Latin, 13 May 1968. Photograph.

representation or what is real, was a source for Caroline de Bendem's emulation, drawing as she did from the historical model to invest the instant of the photograph with a symbolic weight of a certain kind.

> "Instinctively I sat up, my face became more serious and my gestures more solemn. Above all else I wanted to be beautiful and give movement to the representation that was as special as the moment itself. Basically I was posing and I was trapped by the pose. Because all of a sudden I was overcome by emotion : the crowd that was gathering, the justice, the passion, the light, all their banners and the heavy symbol I was carrying at arm's length... I became exactly what I was trying to represent. I was no longer playing a role, I was part of the movement and of the moment, me, the upper-crust English girl, aware of my responsibility." [12]

The interest in this photograph lies in the way it amalgamates the actuality of the event and the historical reference. Never would it have had such an impact on the people of the time – it may not even have been taken – without referring to the painting. The aftermath of the event – which, as has been said, is an important part of the event itself – is, as here, inseparable from the collective memory which is imbued with the example of a previous model. *Marianne of May 68* is not therefore, " a current event devoid of history ". This picture

12 op. cit., p. 75. However, in having sought to make use of the presence of the photographers and to concentrate in a single instant both the movement of the revolt itself and the symbol of the Revolution, the Marianne of the barricades will be disinherited by an indignant grandfather outraged by her conduct.

– which owes its fame to massive mediatisation and to its insertion in the great communication systems – testifies to an event in which the actuality exceeds the limits of the instant itself. Thus, certain images become long-lasting thanks to others that went before. They inherit and revive history, as it were, through the event. The fact that some of these pictures summon up pictorial references is beside the point because it is neither in the historical allusion nor in the iconographical reminder that the true novelty lies. It is, rather, in the power that images have to create a lasting event – and not only a current event – that a new representation of the event, if not of history, becomes possible.

To wish to sum up the century with photographs, as though the most outstanding pictures of the time reveal the most significant events of the same period, shows how important this medium has become in strengthening the basis of the collective memory. If the documentaries and archive films have also played a considerable role in the narration of the century, the photographic image is still prevalent in the efforts undertaken recently to take stock, celebrate and mourn the 20th Century. Using photographs as a means to synthesise history is not surprising given the important role that photography has played in documenting almost every historical fact since the second half of the 19th Century. However, the fact that the photograph was chosen as the means for rereading the 20th Century, makes it an authority in terms of the mediatisation of the event. This is probably because photography unites, in a very convincing way, all the questions concerning the event, the catastrophe and the news, which are inseparable from any contemporary concept of history.

It is certainly because photography has asserted the principle according to which there can be no history without the instant.

Vincent Lavoie, is a university lecturer, critic and essayist.

REFLECTIONS FOR A NEW HISTORY OF PHOTOGRAPHY

Carmelo Vega

As a preliminary step in attempting to define what should be the conceptual and methodological parameters on which to found a history of photography, it is necessary to reflect briefly on the ways of writing the history of the medium, or, in other words, on the prevailing models and on the strategies of analysis of the photographic image as a historical phenomenon.

This issue, which is currently arousing an extraordinary level of interest, on the Spanish scene at least, is not exempt from certain paradoxes; first of all, because many of those models (for example, Beaumont Newhall's) were established in their day as an emergency formula for the purpose of organizing a discipline that until then had been without shape or structure. Those proposals that were posited as an immediate initial solution to a specific problem nonetheless ended up as narrow, orthodox patterns, imitated by subsequent generations of researchers working on photography.

A second paradox, more evident in the case of Spain, is the existence of a model of the history of photography without a model (almost always applied at a local or regional level), on top of which a general historical framework is superimposed with the aim of serving as a point of reference. The methodological fragility of many of these studies stems not so much from adopting this reductionist and geographically-limited schema –almost always unconnected to any overall vision– as from shortcomings in the education of the historian. When all is said and done, who produces or has produced the history of photography? The absence of a specialized discipline in the Spanish university environment has meant that the various contributions to the field of the history of photography have come from uninformed perspectives lacking, in certain cases, the appropriate methodological supports.

The work of the historian of photography who, at the present time, considers her or his activity as a task of renewal, needs to start from an in-depth critique of the values sanctioned as the necessary parameters of a history of photography. In this respect, it seems to be relevant to resolve a couple of questions, such as: on what premisses should we regenerate the history of photography? Or, from what standpoint do we validate our position as historians?

The first measure to be taken in this process of decanting a new history of photography would consist in defining with some exactitude the actual object to be included under the generic label of photography, at the same time clarifying the point of view from which we approach this object. In my opinion, it would be not so much a matter of questioning the possibility of photography as a historicizable subject as such, as of the fact of defining what it is about photography that we are interested in historicizing: this is what Régis Durand calls the "possible histories" of photography (the history of the appearance, of the fixing or the reproduction of the photographic image, the history of photography as a technique –procedures, apparatus, optics, formats– or the history of the uses of photography). Even while allowing the theses that endorse the difficulty of giving historical shape to the field of the photographic, we should not forget that photography, by virtue of its very complexity, encompasses a set of phenomena –on the technical as well as on the theoretical and aesthetic level– that in all probability cannot be separated from one another without creating fissures that would alter their meaning. The task of the historian is not only to draw up mere inventories of events and anecdotes or to put together catalogues of the work of individual photographers, nor is it to organize their biographies, nor to compile eloquent quotations, nor to turn history into an evolutionary exposition of stylistic descriptions of photographic images. The exercise of history would consist in giving shape to a set of independent variables that, properly fitted together and interpreted, would offer us the key to understanding the specific mentality and the particular forms of expression of a man in his time.

In this respect, and as an art historian, it seems to me that exclusive or unidirectional models only serve to hinder an overall vision of the phenomenon of photography. As a discipline linked to the analysis of images and as one with a longer and earlier tradition, Art History offers prior methodological experiences and stances which have subsequently been repeated by scholars of photography: ranging from a history conceived as a hagiography of the great names to a history that welcomes all classes of "minor" productions (according to the obsolete terminology still used by some art historians), such as anonymous or amateur photographs; from a history of the technical and material factors to a history of photographic forms; from a history of commitment and ideologies to a history of perception; from an iconography of photographic motifs to a history of photography from the perspective of the aesthetics of reception.

Obviously, this is not to say that historians of photography are obliged to resort to each one of these models of analysis in order to articulate their studies. All of these methodological systems are only possible facets that guarantee a explanation of the whole and serve to enrich an integral reading of photography.

The incorporation of the history of photographic images into the domain of the history of art –understood as the history of images– has frequently been rejected by those who defend photography as an autonomous and differentiated discipline. While this is not the place to ponder this problem in depth, it is indeed worth clarifying a few points. It is true that art historians, up until a few years ago, had felt no need to become familiar with and explore the fundamental values of photography; it functioned only as an illustration of the work of art, as a mere reproduction and not as an image derived from a distinct creative process and as such susceptible to analysis on the part of Art History.

From the field of photography, too, there was frequently a reluctance to accept openly this relationship. Thus, for example, it is necessary to understand the conceptual problems which still existed in the 1950s that Alsina Munné (*Historia de la Fotografía*. Barcelona, 1954) had to face in attempting to define the "notion of photography as art". To speak of art in reference to photography was, for him, synonymous with being "polemical". Could photography, he wondered, place itself, "even if only secondarily", alongside painting, sculpture and poetry? In his opinion, there was a middle ground for photography: a "new zone" located between Fine Art -"absolute arts"- and the applied arts. In spite of this, the leading role which photography has acquired in the last few decades and its involvement in contemporary artistic experiences have caused the history of art to start to look again at photography from a new perspective: photography is now considered not only as an image that has influenced movements and tendencies in art during the last two centuries (the contaminating character of photography, according to some), but also as embodying and summing up in itself the conflictive nature of contemporary art as such. In this sense, and as we have pointed out already on other occasions, photography is a symptom of the transformations which, from the middle of the 19th century, began to take place in the very concept of art.

Strange as it may seem, it is probable that at the present time the history of art may need photography more than photography needs the history of art. In spite of this, when we speak of the history of art as a framework (not the sole framework, but merely a possible framework) for the study of photography as a historical phenomenon, we do so in the conviction that photography, like other iconic forms of expression and creation, is a response in images to the problems and expectations of a particular era; photography –like painting, poetry, cinema or music– is, first and foremost, a declaration of the sensibility of a time. Consequently, if photography is part of the sum of human creative expression, it also shares with other forms of creation the same principles and postulates, the same causes and effects. Thus, photography would be the manner in which –utilizing its own resources and procedures - human beings translates his vision of the world, or in other words, the way in which the world is expressed in photographic terms.

How, then, are we to explain photography as an isolated and non-referential phenomenon, as an autonomous discipline which is self-sufficient and justifiable in its own terms. According to this version, photography and its history could only be explained in any coherent way by the photographer in person (a fragile means of ensuring an absolute autonomy: history makes it the subject of its own history). In opposition to the purist isolation of photography, I would regard an interconnected relationship with other simultaneous expressions of the creation of images as much more productive, without this implying a renunciation of everything that makes photography distinctively what it is. In short, I believe it is possible to have an Art History which is capable of taking on the study of photography without questioning its specificity, valuing in a positive sense –as an attribute and not a defect– what makes it different from other images is, and adapting the conceptual, formal and terminological contributions specific to photography to the analysis of contemporary art.

Perhaps one of the most interesting contributions made by photography to the debate on artistic creation revolves around the concept of the artist. We are referring here not only to the dialectic derived from the relation established between the creator and the technological mechanism which significantly modifies the role traditionally assigned to the artist. Rather, we are interested in this problem to the extent to which it also has a bearing on certain methodological positions when it comes to engaging with a history of photography. Rosalind Krauss, for example, questions the application of concepts such as artist and artwork in the sphere of photography, citing a number of paradigm cases which invite us to reflect on the dilemma of putting forward a history of photography from the perspective of a history of photographers or a history of images.

With reference to the artist, Krauss mentions the case of certain individuals in the 19th century who were only photographers for a short part of their lives –"can you imagine someone being an artist for only one year?"– and gave it up almost immediately, yet in spite of this they are now depicted as key figures in any history of photography. In this context, it would be useful to reconsider the way in which the historian organizes the recovering of a photographer's work, in order to avoid certain excesses and errors of judgement; it is quite often the case, for example, that photographers whose work is strictly second-rate or of only minor importance are rediscovered and presented (for reasons of ignorance, of a lack of a overall vision, or of vested interest) as if they were creators of unquestionable value, or that, in the attempt to adapt their work to certain dominant discourses, the original intention of the photographer is distorted.

We all know that the photographer's archive is a space of accumulation, and, in most cases, of disorder: there we find photographic materials of all sorts, in a variety of formats and supports, all of them potentially cataloguable objects, but objects that need to be filtered by the specialist if they are not to produce major distortions in the reading of the photographer's work (what is to be done, for example, with the same negative copied by the author himself using different procedures or on different occasions in the course of his life; what is to be done with photographs thrown away or rejected by the photographer; or, as Krauss points out, how are we to distinguish and evaluate the work done by the studio assistants and not by the photographer himself, and how are we to evaluate the ''unfinished'' works?). Furthermore, in every historical examination of the body of photographic material there is an additional quantitative problem that tends to confuse the researcher: it is common for the photographer's archive to be made up of thousands (or tens of thousands) of photographs, many of them realized with a meaning and for a purpose different from those that the contemporary observer looks for and interprets. A rigorous practice of the history of photography would thus entail an adapting of the historian's vision to the original vision of the photographer, something that is only partially possible, given that a history lacking in a certain critical spirit ends up as a mere chronicle devoid of content. This is, indeed, a danger –a methodological virus– that is always associated with the photographic image, and which at times causes the history of photography to lose its way and become an illustrated history of images of the past: in order to create a true history of photography, it is necessary to look at photographs without nostalgia.

From a different point of view, even though it may appear to contradict the one outlined above, we have to admit that photography as a historical phenomenon is subject to a profound ignorance, not only on the part of the general public, but also on the part of the specialists. In effect, what do we really know about the history of photography? It is not only the way in which we experience photography (almost always through reproductions), but the fact that a great number of the images which almost all of us associate with the history of the medium come from the context of particular museums or collections, and are thus affected by the dynamic of the mechanisms that habitually serve to mythologize certain photographers or those of their works in the possession of a given museum or collection: the photograph thus becomes a piece, an object which the institution is interested in making more widely known, and this constant dissemination ends up converting it into a "masterpiece", a classic of photography. In line with the model established by writers such as Gernsheim or Newhall (themselves curators, the former of the Gernsheim Collection at the University of Texas in Austin, and the latter of both the photography department of the Museum of Modern Art in New York and the George Eastman House collection), recent publishing ventures put forward an organization of the history of photography on the basis of the material available in the holdings of certain museums and collections; thus, for example, two recent books for a general readership from the publishing house Taschen (*20th Century Photography* and *Photography from 1839 to Today*) put together their histories of photography from the material in the archives of the Ludwig Museum in Cologne and those of the George Eastman House in Rochester.

Another significant element of distortion in certain histories of photography, especially those by French and English-speaking writers, is the evidently national character of their content, in giving a specially significant role, both in the first moments of the emergence of photography and in the subsequent course of events, to photographers from their own country. This approach, reductionist yet again, imposes itself as a model for other places: the other histories of photography –those of the countries that took up the inventions and proposals of the French and British– seem to make sense only in relation to the work produced in or from those countries. The formula is copied, or the guidelines for an explanation of the history of photography are followed; what is lacking is the critical spirit, the revolt against the imposed model, the revision of the criteria of analysis; in short, what is lacking is a new history of photography.

Carmelo Vega, is a professor at the Universidad de La Laguna and historian.

THE PHOTOGRAPHY OF HISTORY - THE HISTORY OF PHOTOGRAPHY. SOME PERIPHERAL OBSERVATIONS

Hubertus von Amelunxen

There is no history of photography, nor any singularization of the plurality of the history of photography that could lead to a history of the medium, in the sense of an uninterrupted historical continuum or of a linear development. In fact, with the invention of photography each and every one of the visions of the world constituted on a Marxist or capitalist belief in progress ought to have been exploded. Photography is the art of disintegration, of dissemination, according to Jaques Derrida. The union of the atomized referents of the media has been marking the path of the history of photography from the middle of the past century up to the present day, and has done so as a total historical amalgam. Michel Frizot, the editor of the *Nouvelle Histoire de la Photographie* (Bordas, 1995) proves to be one of the few exceptions. This work is the fruit of the labours of a group of authors who offer us a historical vision of the history of photography in which the different themes serve to put forward different points of view. Looking through my bookshelves I find works which deal with photography as a history of the technique, as a history of the art or even of the photographers, as a history of the images, as a history of the styles, as a history of continental, national, urban or regional photography. Ultimately these histories are not distinguishable from those of the other arts. From time to time however, I come across a history of the history. Walter Benjamin, for example, wanted his *Kleine Geschichte der Photographie* (Brief History of Photography) to be seen as a history of the history in which the absolutely definitive nature of a photographic image was set in relation to the history being constructed. This paradox, which Roland Barthes also discusses in, his book *La chambre claire, Note sur la photographie* (Gallimard/Seuil, 1980), can be summed up in one sentence: The photograph is the end result of a process that nevertheless holds the final outcome in suspense. Photography is the art of suspense, it is the art of the threshold *par excellence* – it is a true art of the decision. Nowadays, with photography having achieved social recognition and managed to gain a place in the museums, photography's very capacity to transmit history is itself in danger. Having gained admission to the museum archives, its status as an indicator falls victim to the indices of photographers and styles established by particular collection.

 What is the position of photography today? Is it still possible to speak of photography, or has this medium —whose invention (we might think here of Fox Talbot) gave rise to a process of de-hierarchizing within the representational arts— been complacently relegated, by way of the commodification of art, to the categories of art and non-art? The fact is that photography is allotted practically no space —either in schools or universities— for the teaching of its techniques or its history or its theory, with only a few exceptions which serve to prove the rule. However, a large part of the transmission and reception of such knowledge is based on a unilateral understanding of photography as document or as falsification. Be that as it may, here the concept of falsification has its origin in a mistaken heuristics of photography.

In Berlin they are currently thinking of setting up a centre which will bring together all the cities existing collections. The initial estimates have calculated holdings of approximately 13,000 photographs from a variety of thematic fields: anthropology, ethnology, medicine, criminology, archaeology, Egyptology, Islamic studies, road traffic, architecture, civil and military aviation, the world of publishing, etc.. And also art., with images from collections set up with the specific aim of accumulating photographs of artworks. In these millions of instants in time people, objects and architecture coincide and constitute between them an imaginary museum of realities which have very little in common and yet are also somehow familiar. The digital medium could place this historical material in a present-day context, less as a technique of the image than as a technique of the archive. Only one question arises here: once the process of digital archiving of these photographs has been set in motion, what will the criteria of organization be? The distinction made by Roland Barthes, in what he defined the *studium* as a cultural paradigm and the *punctum* as personal feeling or wound, may perhaps be of some use here, and also for a future historiography of photography. In the first case the determining factor is the intentional gaze of photography; in the second the gaze is assailed by something within the image. The distinction between an appreciation that is codified, supra-individual, social and ideological, and one that is subjective and psychologically motivated will, in my opinion, come to be of essential importance. If we are to arrive at a third level of the archive, the *punctum* and the *studium* must —while conserving their elemental differences— establish a common ordered background that will consist in the subject of the contemplator and will as a matter of principle situate the subject in the strangeness of the world. Once we find ourselves on this path it will become possible for photography to serve as the basis for the emergence of a science of the image, one that could not be classified within any of the existing humanistic disciplines and would therefore, like psychoanalysis, need to be regarded as a metascience. In the same way that photography can show us how to deal with images, psychoanalysis helps us to understand the significance and the consequences of the penetration of the human body by the taking of a photograph. Both photography and psychoanalysis belong to the 19th century. Nevertheless, it has not been until now, at the beginning of the 21st century, that we have begun to harvest the fruits of its legacy.

Hubertus von Amelunxen, is an essayist, writer and curator of exhibitions, and fomer director of the Forum Muthesius in Kiel.

PHOTOGRAPHY, LABORATORY OF A HISTORY OF MODERNITY

André Gunthert

In the recent past, few fields have expanded to the same extent as the study of photography. In the early 1980's in France, the School of Photography in Arles and the CNP (Centre National de la Photgraphie) were set up and the *Mois de la Photo* and the *Cahiers de la photographie* came into being. Nevertheless, anyone who took an interest in photography only had a short list of disparate texts to work with, which went from a survey by a group of sociologists and a thesis on photography to a few journalistic or semiotic essays. In the history section were two exhibition catalogues which were quickly unobtainable[1].

A decade later, this index had grown ten-fold and the research materiel that it contained was much broader and more ambitious, comprising three magazines, several substantial theoretical works as well as a number of catalogues published for the 150th Anniversary – but it still fit into a single shelf of the library. At the turn of the 21st Century, the curve became exponential, revealing a profound change in this domain: the multiplication factor now has three numbers ; each year brings its load of rich spoils in terms of

1 This text was presented at the opening conference of the convention "The history of photography revisited" 19th May, 2000 in Barcelona.

Cf. respectively : Pierre Bourdieu (dir.), Un art moyen, Paris, Minuit, 1965; Gisèle Freund, Photography and Society, Paris, Le Seuil,1974; Susan Sontag, On Photography, Paris, Anchor Books/Doubleday (reprint edition),1990 Roland Barthes, La Chambre claire, Paris, ed. de l,Étoile, Gallimard/Le Seuil, 1980; Bernard Marbot, Une invention du XIXe siècle :la photographie, Paris, Bibliothèque nationale, 1976; Michel Frizot, É.-J. Marey, 1830-1904. La photographie du mouvement, Paris, CGP/MNAM, 1977.

publications, information and new pictures ; research methods are being revised and nourished by closer links with other fields of knowledge ; finally, beyond the limits of this specialisation, the questions posed by photography are spreading and enriching a whole variety of other areas, be they aesthetic, historical, literary or philosophical.

Of course, the works do not all come up to the same standard, but it is enough to compare the number of the publications, and the interest they arouse, with those of many other university specialisations – particularly in the domains of the arts, philosophy or history of art – to see that the study of photography is faring very well. From within a given discipline, it is hard to see anything other than the bad points, the difficulties and the hurdles, but I think we should delight in the distance already covered : from a history of photography perceived by most as a mere annex to the history of art, in its most traditional sense, with its great masters and major works, from autonomist and specialised texts, even if they were written by amateurs (I mean by people who despite their passionate interest, had had no training in this domain), we have progressed to a history that is finally beginning to merit being called scientific, that is much more open and methodological from the theoretical point of view and is expounded by real specialists.

We are doubtlessly still at the start of this new process and are only just beginning to perceive the first fruits and a few scattered signs of it. But I think that these are signs of an undeniable involvement in a process that holds great promise for the years ahead. In my opinion, we are at the very point where the foundations are being laid down and a new history of photography is emerging, one that is not just an historical account of a limited number of works, which only collectors and a few informed amateurs are interested in, but one that extends well beyond the confines of photography and which sees photography as both a practice and a culture : a history that I am tempted to call a *history of the photographic*, rich in its repercussions on both our general understanding of the mechanisms involved in representation, in the fields of art and the modern media, and even on the renewal of the very methodologies used by historians themselves.

This renewal has many reasons which could be analysed (the institutionalisation of photography, its development in to relation art or quite simply the appearance of new funds and materials). Rather than dwelling on this aspect, which would be more appropriate to taking stock of the situation, I would like to move on from attesting to this emergence to querying the conditions for future research and to attempt to point out a few directions that are being taken in an area that is still difficult to clearly discern.

The first thing to consider is the institutional framework. Indeed, the domain of photographic studies is currently in the paradoxical position of being much more active, with regards to research, exhibitions and publications, than many other university specialisations, but still has far to go to acquire the same recognition in the academic institution or the museum. There is a growing disparity between research and the conditions in which the latter is being carried out. Whereas the distance never stops growing between the work being produced by researchers today and the amateurism of the past, the framework in which the work is done is often more akin to that of the self-taught, with its haphazard discovery of resources and the kind of militancy that is inseparable from amateur investigations. Such endearing characteristics have gone as far as they can and are limiting in terms of in-depth analysis, broad-based exploration or the gauging of one's work with regard to scientific production. The researchers' willingness is not in doubt here : what must be appealed to from now on is institutional responsibility – the university first of all, since no research programme can develop over the long term without such support; secondly, the institutions that house the nation's heritage must give researchers access to the materials necessary for their investigations.

The great strides taken by this specialisation, no less than the quality of the works produced in academic circles or for museums, make it possible to state quite clearly that : it is increasingly unacceptable to see students having to make do with invisible directors of study, to see curators discovering photography only when they are given funds to manage, or exhibition commissioners who are surprised by the conditions that the presentation of this medium requires. Reducing the gap no longer depends on the enthusiasm or staunch support of a few individuals but on the contientiousness of those who bear responsibility for the various institutions – which also means a certain amount of lobbying by people who are actors working within the institutions.

Hence, several problems arise, the first of which is the problem of how this discipline should be defined. Should photography become a subject in its own right, as was the case for cinema studies, with its own curriculum, diplomas and professors,? Or should it become part of an existing discipline at the risk of becoming instrumental? If the institutional difficulties are put to one side, there are a number of arguments in favour of the creation of an autonomous discipline: to start with is the relatively autonomous character of the photographic act itself but in addition to this, and above all else, are the complexity and heterogeneity of the problems that are inherent to the study of photography since it covers such a wide range of different historical fields, from art, science and technology to sociology, economics and culture. This solution may be appealing but, for at least three reasons, I do not think it is the best option. In the first place because there are already certain autonomous spaces where photography is taught, such as the National School of Photography in Arles, which have shown that it is difficult, on an institutional level, to separate photographic theory from practical courses. Please don't got me wrong, I do not mean that such courses are illegitimate (and the school in Arles is shining proof of how successful the combination of theory and practice can be) quite to the contrary, they are almost too legitimate to be avoided. But the creation of photographic theory as a specialisation would, I feel, be working towards a different goal. Secondly, the example of cinema studies has shown that autonomy is no guarantee against instrumentality. After a relatively brilliant take off, these courses are now stagnating to a certain extent and in some French faculties they are slowly being annexed to literary departments. Elsewhere, this example reveals that autonomy can engender a real risk of becoming introverted and cut off from the rest of the world. I would not like to appear too critical of colleagues working in the departments of cinema studies, but it seems to me that their work no longer provides the kind of input to the various fields of knowledge that it did in the 1980's. Now this is where my third reason lies, because I think that photography studies, to the contrary, have a great deal to contribute to the different domains covered by history and the social sciences. The magazine *Études photographiques* for instance, was designed precisely as an occasion for inter-disciplinary convergence and discussion, welcoming articles from a variety of different backgrounds, from the history of art or literature to the history of science, aesthetics or contemporary history itself. It seems to me that this proposition is coherent with the field opened up by photography, which I perceive as a real crossroads of methodologies, a much-needed junction where diverse but related questions can be exchanged and that can enrich the different domains for which dialogue is a necessity. It is impossible in photography, unless totally artificial, to set up impervious boundaries between aesthetic and social practices or between technological experimentation and the imaginary or symbolic : the questions raised by photography lead naturally to interdisciplinarity, to the confrontation of different points of view and to the exploration of areas hitherto unknown. I think this is both a strength and a source of great potential and explains perhaps why the study of photography is in vogue today, why students and researchers intuitively see in it the opportunity to experience the interdisciplinarity that the academic programmes boast and that is still so difficult to put into practice.

The definition of this field as a crossroads and meeting-point raises the issue of its integration with the institution. Once it has been acknowledged that it must be integrated somehow, a close examination must be undertaken of the disciplines that are liable to participate in this. Currently, research work into the history of photography falls roughly under the umbrella of three fields : the study of literature, the history of art and communications studies. The choice of one discipline or the other is not without importance. If the situation in France, where work on photography is mostly carried out within the field of the history of art, is compared to the situation in Germany, where they are absorbed by *Medienwissenschaft* (media sciences), the result are not the same. In Germany, the history of art is somewhat conservative and has not yet integrated photography, forcing students who wish to study it to turn to other specialisations. Since communications studies involves little history or training in image analysis, the students tend to produce aesthetic or theoretical demonstrations that are of a general nature and which privilege the message to the detriment of an analysis of its formal representation. Consequently, few works on the history of photography are produced in Germany today and the quality of the works that are published there is mediocre. In France, the fact that certain departments of the history of art have admitted photography, has led to better results even if, here too, students tend to be attracted increasingly by communications studies. This trend gives me leave to address a warning to the heads of these history departments : as in nature, research hates a vacuum, and if the history of art is incapable of opening up and offering the proper training at a pace that responds to the demand, other specialisations will take its place.

Of course, the integration of the history of photography with the history of art implies that the latter undergo a major overhaul and that even its title be queried, since the practice of photography is only partially dependant on questions specific to art. However, the history of art is unavoidable as it alone can provide training in the methodologies necessary for the analysis of the image, and it seems to me that it should consider the integration of photography as a chance and opportunity for renewal that will not only extend its field of inquiry but will also increase the interest it arouses. To tell the truth, unless the history of art slowly becomes extinct, I think it is bound to turn into a general history of representations (artistic and non-artistic) in which photography will play a major role. In a few words, the development that I advocate is two-fold : the history of photography becoming the history of the photographic and the history of art becoming the history of representation. Far from being Utopian, this kind of project, I feel, is indicative of a need for change, a change that certain signs are already pointing to.

What must be considered next is the question of theory. First of all I must say that, on the methodological level, I find it difficult to be as clear-cut here as my opinions are with regard to the institution. The practice of photography covers such a vast field that we are only just beginning to appreciate how rich and varied it is – a field that is much more complex and especially less homogenous than, say, Renaissance painting. Just as the practicians in the 19th Century who, to describe the practice of photography, produced lists of its applications, lists that grew longer and longer with the passing of time and ended up covering almost every social practice, it would be possible to produce a long list of the questions raised by the history of photography which would end up covering almost every histiographic practice and would become meaningless in as much as methodological options are born and renewed by the very practice of research itself. These considerations make me think that photography is not a *matter* as such, in the sense that the dynamics of liquids is a matter of physics, I mean an object that can be clearly identified and described in detail – which would make it possible to define a fixed set of appropriate methodologies. In fact, after many years practising the history of this medium, I am tempted to describe photography as a point of refraction or projection that inevitably takes us back to the social, cultural or aesthetic practices which provide it with a frame within which to work. This observation indicates very generally, the direction that research could take. To sum it up in a word, this direction – which I do not consider exclusive of other approaches but which may provide a guide for future methodologies - is one that considers the history of photography from the angle of its reception. To choose to found one's analysis on recipient conditions can be justified by two affirmations. Contrary to the essentialist approach that has marked photographic theory since the 1930's, the approach that entails decoding any manifestation from the point of view of its reception stems from the belief that the mechanisms at work are tied wholly to an economy of representation and refuses any form of instrumental fatality. If the technical question plays a preponderant role, it must always be seen as part of a cultural process, in terms of how it is perceived at a particular time and within a given society. This observation must be completed by a remark relating to the field itself and the way it functions : the development of the imagination around the instrumental production of images places the evolution of figurative systems, for the most part, upon the criteria relative to their reception. What does the photograph's title tell us? Contrary to manual representations or reproductions in print, these images have neither an author nor an original – or else have no author other than the machine, no original other than the optical projection. Although the instrumentality on which they depend is the fruit of human activity, and despite the fact that the mechanics reflect the choices of the producer, the automatisation that conditions their appearance, confronts the actors of representation with a totally new form of distancing. In other words, even for their maker, the only space that these images allow for their comprehension, is that of their reception.

As a motive for the abundance of technical images, this characteristic may hold the key to their analysis. Until today, the main approaches to contemporary iconography were subject to the apparently logical, but somewhat paradoxical, temptation to draw up, according to technical determinations, specialised cultural divisions (the history of photography, of the cinema, of television, of the press, of advertising, of propaganda, of the comic strip, of the digital image etc.). Despite the numerous points at which they converge, these heterogeneous approaches have been unable to produce a satisfactory blueprint that explains this phenomenon and that is characteristic of contemporary times i.e. the unprecedented growth in the production and use of images. By taking the emphasis off the technical side and placing it on the social, a history of reception is doubly interesting in that it leads to a global description of image production in the 19th and 20th Centuries that can be placed in no uncertain terms under the banner of the social sciences. As such, the history of photography could quite simply become the laboratory of a history of modernity. I couldn't wish it a worse fate than that!

André Gunthert is a historian, university lecturer and editor of the magazine *Études Photographiques*.

HISTORY OF PHOTOGRAPHY
Selected bibliography

Mariona Fernández

This bibliographical summary is concerned with generic studies of the history of photography. It takes no account of works that deal exclusively with a single country, but it does include those that study genres or movements, and those that make reference to one or other of the themes that have traditionally attracted photographers, such as landscape, nude, portrait, architecture and movement, or techniques such as photomontage which constitute a genre. Reference books, encyclopaedias, magazines and monographs devoted to an individual photographer have also been ommitted. Although the contributing experts have suggested books of essays of evident interest, these are not cited in this bibliography, falling as they do outside the scope of the general historical study that is our intention here.

The bibliographical entries have been drawn from a variety of sources, and have not been compiled by direct consultation of the document in question. Wherever the available information so permitted, each entry contains the following data: author or editor, title, city, publisher and year of publication.

We have attempted to list the various editions of a given title, particularly in the case of works translated from other languages or revised and expanded editions.

The selection has been made on the basis of consultation with the following individuals, whose initials appear after each quotation:

(HvA)   Hubertus von Amelunxen
(DG)   Daniel Girardin
(I.J)   Ian Jeffrey
(BK)   Boris Kossoy
(AK)   Andrea Kunard
(JN)   Joan Naranjo
(MLS)   Marie-Loup Sougez
(JS)   Johan Swinnen
(CV)   Carmelo Vega

We have taken the three books most frequently cited by this group of authorities, and have added a number of titles cited in the bibliographies of the works in question. Their initials also appear at the end of each bibliographical entry.

(MF) FRIZOT, Michel (Ed.). *Nouvelle Histoire de la Photographie*. Paris : Bordas, 1994. (From the bibliography compiled by Fred and Elisabeth Pajerski.)

(BN) NEWHALL, Beaumont. *Historia de la Fotografia desde sus or'genes hasta nuestros dias.* Barcelona, Gustavo Gili, 1983. (This bibliography from the Spanish translation is based on the 5th edition of the book published by the MoMA, which is significantly different from the 1949 edition.)

(L/R) LEMAGNY, Jean Claude and André ROUILLÉ (ed); *Historia de la fotografia*. Barcelona: Ediciones Mart'nez Roca, 1988. (Critical bibliography.)

To these we have been added a number of titles which we felt it important to include in this study.
Mariona Fernández

ADES, Dawn. *Photomontage.* New York: Pantheon Books, 1976; New York; London: Thames and Hudson, 1986; Paris: La Chêne, 1978. *Fotomontaje.* Barcelona: Bosch Casa Editorial SA, 1977 (BN) (L/R)

ALSINA i MUNNƒ, Ermengol. *Historia de la fotografía* / in conjunction with Juan-Eduardo Cirlot. Barcelona: Producciones editoriales del Nordeste, 1954

AMAR, Pierre-Jean. *Histoire de la Photographie.* Paris: Presses Universitaires de France, 1997

AMAR, Pierre-Jean. *La Photographie, histoire d'un art.* Aix-en-Provence: Édisud, 1993

BAATZ, Willfried. *Photography* / with a foreword by L. Fritz Gruber. London: Laurence King, 1999

BAIER, Wolfgang. *Quellendarstellungen zur Geschichte der Fotografie.* Halle: Fotokinoverlag, 1965; Munich: Schirmer / Mosel, 1977 (BN) (MF)

BALLONE, Roger. *La photographie*. Paris: Presses Universitaires de France, 1996

BAQUE, Dominique. *Les documents de la modernité: Anthologie de textes sur la photographie, de 1919 à 1939*. Nîmes: Jacqueline Chambon, 1993 (DG) (MF)

BARTRAM, Michael. *The Pre-Raphaelite Camera. Aspects of Victorian Photography*. London: Weidenfeld & Nicolson, 1985 (MF)

BEATON, Cecil / Gail BUCKLAND. *The Magic Image: The Genius of Photography from 1839 to the Present Day*. Boston; Toronto: Little, Brown & Co., 1975; London: Weidenfeld & Nicolson, 1975 (BN) (MF)

BELLONE, Roger / Luc FELLOT. *Histoire mondiale de la photographie en couleurs*. Paris: Hachette-Realités, 1981 (L/R)

BENJAMIN, Walter. *Kleine geschichte der photographie*. S.l.: Die Literaische Welt, 1931; *Petite histoire de la Photographie*. In: Poésie et *Révolution*. Paris: D'noel, 1971; *Pequeña historia de la fotografia*. In: Discursos interrumpidos.

Madrid: Taurus, 1982*; Breve historia de la fotografia*. In: Archivos de la Fotografia, vol. II, nœm. 2. Zarautz: Photomuseum, 1997 (CV) (JN) (HvA) (MLS) (DG)

BENJAMIN, Walter. *L'oeuvre d'art à l'ère de sa reproductibilité technique*. In: Poésie et Révolution. Paris: Denoël, 1971 (1st ed. 1936); *La obra de arte en la época de su reproducibilidad técnica*. A: Archivos de la Fotografia, vol. II, nœm. 2. Zarautz: Photomuseum, 1997 (DG) (MLS)

BERNARD, Bruce. *Photodiscovery: Masterworks of Photography 1840-1940*. New York: Harry N. Abrams, 1980. (BN)

BERTONATI, Emilio. *Das experimentelle Photo in Deustchland 1918-1940*. Munich: Galleria del Levante, 1978

BILLETER, Erika. *Malerei und Photographie im Dialog*. Berna: Bentelli, 1977

BOLTON, Richard (Ed.). *The Contest of Meaning: Critical Histories of Photography*. Cambridge: MIT Press, 1989 (AK) (MF)

BORHAN, Pierre. *Voyons voir.* Paris: Creatis, 1980

Botanica. Photographies de végétaux aux XIXe et XXe siècles. Paris: Centre National de la Photographie, 1987 (MF)

BOURDIEU, Pierre. *Un art moyen.* Paris: Éd. de Minuit, 1965 (L/R)

BRAIVE, Michel. *L'Âge de la photographie de Niépce à nos jours.* Bruxelles: Ed. de la Connaissance, 1965 (L/R) (MF)

BUCKLAND, Gail. *Reality Recorded: Early Documentary Photography.* Greenwich (Connecticut): New York Graphic Society, 1974 (MF)

BUCKLAND, Gail. *Fox Talbot and the invention of Photography.* Boston: David R. Godine, 1980

BUDDEMEIR, Heinz. *Panorama, Diorama, Photographie: Ensttehung und Wirkung neuer Medien im 19. Jahrhundert.* Munich: Wilhelm Fink, 1970 (MF)

BUNNELL, Peter (Ed.). *A Photographic Vision: Pictorial Photography 1889-1923.* Salt Lake City (Utah): Peregrine Smith, 1980 (BN)

BURNS ARCHIVE. *Masterpieces of medical photography: Selections from Burns Archive.* Pasadena: Twelvetrees, 1987

CAFFIN, Charles H. *Photography as Fine Art: The Achievement and Possibilities of Photographic Art in America.* (original edition 1901). Dobbs Ferry (NY): Morgan & Morgan, 1971 (BN)

CHEVRIER, Jean François and James LINGWOOD. *Une autre objectivité = Another Objectivity.* Milano: Idea Books, 1989 (MF)

CHIARAMONTE, Giovanni. *The Story of Photography: an illustrated history.* New York: Aperture, 1983

CHRIST, Yvan. *L'Âge d'or de la photographie.* Paris: Vincent, Fréal et Cie, 1965 (MF)

COE, Brian. *The Birth of Photography: The Story of Formative Years 1800-1900.* London: Ash & Grant, 1976 (MF)

COKE, Van Deren. *The Painter and Photograph from Delacroix to Warhol.* Albuquerque: University of New Mexico Press, 1964; 2nd ed. 1972 (BN)

COKE, Van Deren (Ed.). *One hundred years of photographic history: essays in honor of Beaumont Newhall*. Albuquerque: University of New Mexico Press, 1975

COLLINS, Kathleen. *Shadow and Substance: Essays on the History of Photography in honor of Heinz K. Henish*. Troy (Michigan): The Amorphous Institute Press, 1990

Conférences publiques sur la photographie: Théorique et technique: organisées sous l'egide de la Societé Française de Photographie et du Conservatoire national des Arts et métiers: 1891-1900. Paris: Jean-Michel Place, 1987

Contemporary Photographer. New York: Macmillan Publishers Co., 1982 (L/R)

COOPER, Thomas / Paul HILL. *Dialogue with photography*. New York: Farrar, 1979

CRAWFORD, William. *The Keepers of Light: A History & Working Guide to Early Photographic Processes*. Dobbs Ferry (NY): Morgan & Morgan, 1979 (BN)

DANZIGER, James. *Interviews with master photographers.* New York: Paddington, 1977

DARRAH, William C. *The World of Stereography*. Gettysburg (Pennsylvania): William C. Darrah, 1977 (BN)

DAVAL, Jean-Luc. *La photographie: histoire d'un art.* Genève : Skira, 1982 (L/R)

DAVENPORT, Alma. *The History of photography: an overview*. Boston, etc.: Focal, 1991

DELPIRE, Robert. *Histoire du voir ; une histoire de la photographie...* / text by Michel Frizot. Evreux: Centre National de la Photographie, 1994

DOTY, Robert. *Photo-Secession: Stieglitz and the Fine Art Movement in Photography*. New York: Dover Publications, 1978 (BN)

DURAND, Régis. *El tiempo de la imagen. Ensayo sobre las condiciones de una historia de las formas fotográficas.* Salamanca: Ediciones Universidad de Salamanca, 1998 (CV)

EAUCLAIRE, Sally. *The New Color Photography*. New York: Abbeville Press, 1981 (L/R)

EDER, Josef Maria. *Quellenschriften zu den frühsten Anfängen der Photographie bis zum XVIII. Jahrhundert.* Halle: s.n., 1913; New York: Arno, 1979 (MF)

EDER, Josef Maria / Edward EPSTEIN. *Geschichte der Photographie.* Halle: W. Knapp, 1932 (1st ed. Berlin, 1905); *History of Photography.* New York, Columbia University, 1945; New York: Arno, 1979; New York: Dover, 1978. (BN) (JS) (L/R) (MF) (DG)

EDWARDS, Elizabeth (Ed.). *Antropology and Photography 1860-1920.* London; New Haven, Yale University Press, 1992 (JN) (MF)

FIEDLER, Jeannine (Ed.). *Photography at the Bauhaus.* London: Dirk Nishen Publishing, 1990

FONTCUBERTA, Joan (Ed.). *Estética fotográfica. Una selección de textos.* Barcelona: Editorial Blume, 1984
Fotografi 150 ar: svensk och utländsk fotografi ca 1840-1989 ur museets samlingar. Stockholm: Moderna Museet, 1989
Fotografie 1922-1982 = Photography 1922-1982 ("Photokina" Weltmesse Der Fotografie, 1982.) / Photokina World Fair Of Photography (1982, Cologne). Cologne. Josef-Haubrich-Kunsthalle, 1982

FREUND, Gisèle. *Photographie et Société.* Paris: Le Seuil, 1974; *Photography and Society.* Boston: David R. Godina, 1980; *La fotografia como documento social.* Barcelona: Gustavo Gili, 1986 (BK) (BN) (CV) (L/R) (MF) (MLS)

FRIZOT, Michel (Ed.). *Nouvelle Histoire de la Photographie.* Paris: Bordas, 1994; *A New History of Photography.* Köln: Könemann, 1998 (AK) (CV) (DG) (HvA) (IJ) (JN) (MLS)

FULTON MARGOLI, Marianne. *Camera Work: A Pictorial Guide.* New York: Dover Publications, 1978 (BN)

GALASSI, Peter. *Before Photography. Painting and the Invention of Photography.* New York: The Museum of Modern Art, 1981 (BN) (MLS)

GASSAN, Arnold. *A Chronology of Photography. A Critical Survey of the History of Photography as a Medium of Arts.* Athens (Ohio): Handbook Company, 1972 (L/R)

Das Gedruckte Photo: Photokina Bilder-schauen / Photokina Bilderschauen (1984, Köln). Köln: Messegelände, 1984

GERNSHEIM, Helmut. *A Concise History of Photography*. New York: Dover, 1986

GERNSHEIM, Helmut. *Creative Photography. Aesthetic Trends 1839.1960*. London: Faber and Faber, 1962 (CV)

GERNSHEIM, Helmut. *The History of Photography: from the Camera Obscura to the Beginning of the Modern Era*. London: McGraw-Hill Book Company, 1969 (1955) (CV) (JS) (BN) (L/R)

GERNSHEIM, Helmut / Alison GERNSHEIM. *Historia gráfica de la Foto grafía*. Barcelona: Ediciones Omega, 1967

GERNSHEIM, Helmut / Alison GERNSHEIM. *The History of Photography: From the Earliest Use of the Camera Obscura in the Eleventh Century up to 1914*. London; New York; Toronto: Oxford University Press, 1955; 2nd ed., New York: McGraw-Hill, 1969; London: Thames and Hudson, 1969; 3rd. Ed.,

revised in 2 vols.: *The Origins of Photography; The Rise of Photography, 1850-1880: the Age of Collodion*. New York; London: Thames and Hudson, 1982; 1988 (MF)

GIDAL, Tim N. *Modern Photojournalism: Origin and Evolution 1910-1933*. New York: Macmillan Publishing Company, 1973 (BN) (MF)

GILARDI, Ando. *Storia sociale della fotografia*. Milano: Feltrinelli, 1981 (JN) (MF) (L/R)

GOLDBERG, Vicki (Ed.). *Photography in Print: Writtings from 1816 to the present*. Albuquerque: University of New Mexico Press, 1981 (AK) (MF) (BN)

GOLDBERG, Vicki. *The Power of Photography: How Photography Changed Our Lives*. New York: Abbeville Press, 1991 (JS)

GOSSIN, H. *La photographie, son histoire, ses procédés, ses applications*. Paris: s.n., 1887 (L/R)
Great Photographic essays from Life. Boston: New York Graphic Society, 1978 (BN)

GREEN, Jonathan. *American History. A Critical History from 1945 to the Present.* New York: Harry N. Abrams, 1984 (L/R)

GRUNDBERG, Andy. *Photography and Art: Interactions since 1946.* New York: Abbeville Press, 1987

GUERRIN, Michel. *Profession photoreporter: vingt ans d'images d'actualité.* Paris: Centre Georges Pompidou; Gallimard, 1988

GUTIÉRREZ ESPADA, Luis. *Historia de los medios audiovisuales: 1838-1926.* Madrid: Pirámide, cop. 1979-1982

HAENDLER, Carl-Albrecht (Ed.). *Dada: Photographie und Photocollage.* Hanovre: Kestner, 1979 (MF)

HALL-DUNCAN, Nancy. *Histoire de la photographie de mode.* Paris: Chêne, 1978

HARKER, Margaret. *The Linked Ring : The Secession Movement in Photography in Britain 1892-1910.* London: William Heinemann, 1979 (BN)

HARRISON, W. Jerome. *A History of Photography.* (1st ed. 1887); New York: Arno Press, 1973 (BN)

HASSNER, Rune. *Bilder för Miljoner.* Stockholm: (RTV), 1977 (L/R)

HEILBRUN, Françoise / Bernard MARBOT / Philippe NEAGU. *L'invention d'un regard (1839-1918).* Paris: Réunion des Musées Nationaux, 1989 (DG) (MF)

HENDRIKS, Klaus B. (Ed.). *Fundamentals of Photograph Conservation: A Study Guide.* S.l.: unnumbered , 1991 (JS)

HENISCH, Heinz K. / Bridget A. HENISCH. *The Photographic Experience: exhibition to celebrate the 150th Anniversary of the Invention of Photography.* University Park, Pa.: Pennsylvania State University Press, 1988; *The Photographic Experience, 1839-1914: images and attitudes.* University Park, Pa.: Pennsylvania State University Press, 1994

HICKS, Wilson. *Words and Pictures: An Introduction to Photojournalism.* (1st. ed. 1952); New York : Arno, 1973. (BN)

HOLME, Charles (Ed.) *Art in Photography, with Selected Examples of European and American WorK.* London: The Studio, 1905 (BN)

HORSLEY HINTON, A. *L'Art Photographique dans le paysage*. Paris: unnumbered, 1894

HURLEY, F. Jack *Portrait of a decade: Roy Stryker and the Development of Documentary Photography in the Thirties*. Baton Rouge: Louisiana State University Press, 1972 (BN)

Image and Memory, photography from Latin America 1866-1994. Houston: Texas University Press, 1998 (BK)

IVINS Jr., W.M., *Imagen impresa y conocimiento*. Barcelona: Gustavo Gili, 1975 (MLS)

JAGUER, Édouard. *Les mystères de la chambre noire*. Paris: Flammarion, 1982 (L/R)

JEFFREY, Ian. *Photography. A Concise History*. London: Thames and Hudson, 1981; *Fotografía: una breve historia*. Barcelona: Destino, 1999 (IJ)

JEFFREY, Ian. *Revisions: An alternative history of photography*. Bradford: The National Museum of Photography, Film and Television, 1999 (IJ)

JUSSIM, Estele. *Landscape as Photograph*. New Haven: Yale, 1955 (L/R)

JUSSIM, Estele. *Visual Communication and the Graphic Arts: Photographic Technologies in the Nineteenth Century*. New York: R. R. Bowker Company, 1974 (BN)

KEIM, Jean-A. *Histoire de la Photographie*. Paris: Presses Universitaires de France, 1970 (Colección *Que sais-je?*); *Historia de la fotografía*. Vilassar de Mar: Oikos-Tau, 1971

KEMP, Wolfgang. *Theorie der Fotografie I. 1839-1912*. Munich: Schimmer / Mosel, 1980; *Theorie der Fotografie II. 1912-1945*. Munich: Schimmer / Mosel, 1979; *Theorie der Fotografie III. 1945 1980*. Munich: Schimmer / Mosel, 1983

KEMPE, Fritz. *Daguerreotypie in Deutschland*. Seebruck am Chiemsee: Heering-Verlag, 1979 (BN)

KOPPEN, Erwin. *Literatur und Photographie: über Geschichte und Thematik einer Medienentdeckung*. Stuttgart: J. B. Metzlersche, 1987. (MF)

KOZLOFF, Max. *Photography and Fascination.* Danbury, New Hampshire: Addison House, 1979 (IJ)

KOZLOFF, Max. *The Privileged Eye.* Albuquerque: University of New Mexico Press, 1987 (IJ)

KOZLOFF, Max. *Lone Visions Crowded Frames.* Alburquerque: University of New Mexico Press, 1994 (IJ)

KRACAUER, Siegfried. *Photographie.* S.l. : unnumbered., 1927 (HvA)

KRAUSS, Rosalind. *Le Photographique: pour une théorie des écarts.* Paris: Macula, 1990 (CV) (MF)

KRAUSS, Rosalind i Jane LIVINGSTON. *L'amour fou: Photography & Surrealism.* New York: Abbeville Press, Publishers, 1985; *Explosante-fixe: photographie et surréalisme.* Paris: Centre Georges Pompidou; Hazan, 1985

Künstlerphotographien im XX.Jahrhundert. Kat. Hannover: Kestner-Gesellschaft, 1977

LACAN, Ernest. *Esquisses Photographiques.* Paris: Granart, 1862 (JN)

LACOUE-LABARTHE, Philippe. *Portrait de l'artiste en général.* S.l.: unnumbered, 1979 (HvA)

LASSAM, Robert. *Portrait and the Camera: a Celebration of 150 Years of Photography.* London: Studio, 1989

LÉCUYER, Raymond. *Histoire de la Photographie.* Paris: Baschet, 1945; New York: Arno Press, 1979 (BN) (JN) (L/R) (MF) (MLS)

LEMAGNY, Jean Claude / Alain SAYAG *L'invention d'un art: cent cinquantième anniversaire de la photographie.* Paris: Centre Georges Pompidou; Adam Biro, 1989 (DG)

LEMAGNY, Jean Claude / André ROUILLÉ (Ed.). *Histoire de la Photographie.* Paris: Bordas, 1986; *Historia de la fotografía.* Barcelona: Ediciones Martínez Roca, 1988 (CV) (JS) (BK) (MF)

LEMAGNY, Jean Claude. *Photo creative.* Paris: Contrejour, 1984 (L/R)

LEVINSKI, Jorge. *The Naked and the Nude: a History of Nude Photography.* London: Weidenfeld & Nicolson, 1987 (MF)

LIER, Henri van. *Histoire photographique de la photographie.* S.l.: A.C.C.P., 1992

Life Library of Photography. 17 vols. New York: Time-Life Books, 1970-1972 (BN)

LISTA, Giovanni. *Futurismo e fotografia.* Milano: Multipla, 1980; Paris: Musée d'Art Moderne de la Ville, 1981 (L/R)

LOTHROP, Easton S. Jr. *A century of Cameras from the Collection of the International Museum of Photography at George Eastman House.* Dobbs Ferry (NY): Morgan & Morgan, 1973 (BN)

LONDON, Barbara y Lee D. WITKIN. *The Photograph's Collector's Guide.* Boston: New York Graphic Society, 1979 (JN)

LYONS, Nathan (Ed.). *Photographers on Photography A Critical Anthology.* Englewood Cliffs, NJ; Rochester, NY: Prentice Hall; George Eastman House, 1966 (MF) (BN)

LYONS, Nathan. *Toward a Social Landscape...* New York; Rochester: Horizon Press; George Eastman House, 1966 (BN)

MADDOW, Ben. *Faces: a Narrative History of the Portrait in Photography.* Boston: New York Graphic Society, 1977 (L/R)

MARBOT, Bernard. *Une invention du XIXè siècle: la photographie.* Paris: Bibliothèque Nationale, 1976

MARBOT, Bernard / André ROUILLÉ. *Le corps et son image: photographies du dix-neuvième siècle.* Paris: Contrejour, 1986 (MF)

MASCLET, Daniel. *Le Paysage en Photographie.* Paris: Paul Montel, 1947

MAYER & PIERSON. *La photographie: Considérée comme art et comme industrie.* Paris, Librairie I Hachette et Cia., 1862 (JN)

McCAULEY, Elizabeth Anne. *Industrial Madness: Commercial Photography in Paris, 1848-1871.* New Haven: Yale University Press, 1994 (AK)

MELLOR, David (Ed.). *Germany: The New Photography 1927-1933.* London: Arts Council of Great Britain, 1978 (BN)

MENTIENNE, Adrien. *La découverte de la photographie en 1839.* New York: Arno Press, 1979

MOHOLY, Lucia. *A Hundred Years of Photography.* Harmondsworth: Penguin Books, 1939

MORMORIO, Diego. *Una invenzione fatale: breve genealogia della fotografia.* Palermo: Sellerio Editore, cop. 1985

MZARKOVA, Daniela. *Masters of Photography: A Thematic History.* Northants (GB): Hamlyn Books, 1987

NADEAU, Louis. *Encyclopedia of Printing. Photographic and Photomechanical Processes.* New Brunswick: Louis Nadeau, 1994 (JS)

NAEF, Weston J. *The Collection of Alfred Stieglitz: Fifty Pioneers of Modern Photography.* New York: The Metropolitan Museum of Art; The Viking Press, 1979 (BN)

NAEF, Weston J. *Era of Exploration: The Rise of Landscape Photography in the American West 1860-1885.* Buffalo (NY); New York : Albright-Knox Art Gallery; The Metropolitan Museum of Art, 1975 (BN)

NEWHALL, Beaumont. *The Daguerreotype in America.* New York: Dover Publications, 1976 (BN)

NEWHALL, Beaumont. *The History of Photography from 1839 to the Present.* New York: MoMA, 1949; *L'Histoire de la photographie, depuis 1839 a nos jours.* Paris: Belier-Prisma, 1967; *The History...* London: Seker and Warburg, 1982; *Historia de la Fotografia desde sus orígenes hasta nuestros dias.* Barcelona: Gustavo Gili, 1983 (DG) (HvA) (JS) (L/R) (MF) (MLS)

NEWHALL, Beaumont. *Latent Image: The Discovery of Photography.* Garden City, NY: Doubleday & Co. 1967; Albuquerque: University of New mexico Press, 1983 (MF)

NEWHALL, Beaumont. *Photography 1839-1937.* New York: The Museum of Modern Art, 1937 (JN) (the basic catalogue for both the 1938 edition and the subsequent 1949 edition)

NEWHALL, Beaumont. *Photography. A short critical history.* New York: The Museum of Modern Art, 1938 (CV) (the basis for the 1949 edition, translated and published in various countries and also reissued by the MoMA)

NEWHALL, Beaumont. *Photography: Essays & Images*. New York: The Museum of Modern Art, 1980 (BN)

On the Art of Fixing a Shadow / various authors. New York: National Gallery of Art; The Art Institute of Chicago, 1989 (MLS)

PALAZZOLI, Daniela. *Combattimento per un'immagine Fotografi e Pittori*. Torino: Galleria Civica d'Art Moderna, 1973

PALMQUIST, Peter. *Photographers: A Sourcebook for Historical Research*. Brownsville, CA: Carl Mautz, 1991 (MF)

PETRUCK, Peninah R. (Ed.). *The Camera Viewed: Writtings on Twentieth-century Photography*, 2 vols., New York: E.P. Dutton, 1979 (BN)

PHILLIPS, Christopher (Ed.). *Photography in the Modern Era: European Documents and Critical Writings, 1913-1940*. New York: The Metropolitan Museum of Modern Art; Aperture, 1989

Photography, Discovery and Invention. Malibu: J. Paul Getty Museum, 1990 (MF)

Photography: The First Eighty Years. London: P. & D. Coinaghi & Co. Ltd., 1976

Photography's beginnings: a Visual History Featuring the Collection of Wm. B. Becker. Oakland: Meadow Brook Art Gallery of Oakland University, 1989

Photomontage: Experimental Photography between the Wars / Centre National de la Photographie, Paris. London: Thames & Hudson, 1991

POLLACK, Peter. *History of Photography: from the Earliest Beginnings to the Present* Day. New York: Harry N. Abrams, 1958 (ed. rev. 1969). *Histoire mondiale de la photographie*. Paris : Hachette, 1961 (L/R) (MF)

POTONNIÉE, Georges. *Histoire de la découverte de la photographie*. Paris: Montel, 1925 (L/R); *History of the Discovery of Photography*. New York: Arno Press, 1973 (BN)

PRITCHARD, H. Baden. *The Photographic Studios of Europe*. London: Piper & Carter, 1882; New York: Arno Press, 1973 (MF)

Reading into Photography. Selected essays 1959-1980 / Thomas F. Barrow,

Shelley Armitage y William E. Tydeman (Ed.). Albuquerque: Universtity of New Mexico Press, 1982
Reality Recorded: Early Documentary Photography. Boston: New York Graphic Society, 1974. (MF)

RECHT, Roland. *La lettre de Humboldt*. Paris: Christian Bourgois, 1989 (MLS)

RIEGO, Bernardo / Carmelo VEGA. *Fotografía y métodos históricos: dos textos para un debate*. Santander; Santa Cruz de Tenerife: Universidad de Cantabria; Universidad de La Laguna, 1994

ROOSENS, Laurent / Luc SALU. *History of Photography: A Bibliography of Books*. London: Mansell, 1989 (JS)
ROOT, M.A. *The Camera and The Pencil: or The Heliographic Art, Its Theory and Practice in all Its Various Branches*. Philadelphy; New York: Root, Lippincott, Appleton, 1864; (reed.) Pawlet : Helios, 1971 (MF)

ROSENBLUM, Naomi. *A World History of Photography*. New York: Abbeville Press, 1984. *Histoire mondiale de la photographie*. Paris: Flammarion, 1992 (L/R) (MF) (MLS)

ROUILLÉ, André. *L'Empire de la photographie: Photographie et Pouvoir Bourgeois, 1839-1870*. Paris: Le Sycomore, 1982. (L/R) (MF)

ROUILLÉ, André. *La photographie en France; textes et controverses: Une anthologie, 1816-1871*. Paris: Macula, 1989 (MF)

ROSENBLUM, Naomi. *A World history of photography*. New York: Abbeville Press, 1989

ROSENBLUM, Naomi. *A History of women photographers*. London; New York: Abbeville Press, 1994

RUDISILL, Richard. *Mirror Image: The Influence of the Daguerreotype on American Society*. Albuquerque: The University of New Mexico Press, 1971

SCHAEFFER, Jean-Marie. *L'Image précaire: du dispositif photographique*. Paris: Le Seuil, 1987 (MF)

SCHARF, Aaron. *Art and Photography*. London: Allen Lane The Penguin Press, 1968; New York: Penguin Books, 1986 (BN) (CV) (L/R)

SEKULA, Alan. *Photography against the Grain: Essays and Photo Works 1973-1983*. S.l. : unnumbered ,1984 (HvA)

SHAW, Bernard / Bill JAY / Margaret MOORE (Ed.). *Bernard Shaw on Photography*. New York: unnumbered, 1849; (republished) Hastings-on-Hudson: Morgan & Morgan, 1970 (MF)

SCHWARZ, Heinrich. *Art and Photography: Forerunners and Influences. Selected Essays*. Rochester, Layton: Visual Studies Workshop and Peregrine Smith, 1985 (MF)

SIPLEY. Louis Walton. *A Half Century of Colour*. New York: The Macmillan Company, 1951 (BN)

SKOPEC, Rudolf. *Photographie im Wandel der Zeiten*. Praga: Artia, 1964 (MF)

SOBIESZEK, Robert A. *The Art of Persuasion: A History of Advertising photography*. New York: Harry N. Abrams, 1988 (MF)

SOLOMON-GODEAU, Abigail. *Photography at the Dock*. Minneapolis: University of Minnesota Press, 1991 (AK)

SORIN, Pierre. *Les Fils de Nadar: Le "siècle" de l'image analogique*. Paris: Nathan, 1997

SOUGEZ, Emmanuel. *La Photographie: son histoire; La photographie: son univers*. Paris: L'Illustration, 1968-1969 (L/R) (MF)

SOUGEZ, Marie-Loup. *Historia de la fotografía*. Madrid: Cátedra, 1985

STELZER, Otto. *Kunst und Photographie. Kontakte Einsflüsse Wirkungen*. München: R. Piper & Co. Verlag, 1966; *Arte y fotografía: contactos, influencias y efectos*. Barcelona: Gili, cop., 1981

STEIN, Ralph. *The pin-up: From 1852 to Now*. New York: The Ridge Press, 1974

STENGER, Erich. *Die Photographie in Kultur und Technik*. Leipzig: E.A. Seemann, 1938; republication of the English version: New York: Arno, 1979 (MF)

STEINORTH, Karl. *Photographen der 20er. Jahre*. Munic: Verlag der Laterna Magica, 1979 (BN)

STORY, Alfred T. *The story of Photography*. New York: McClure Phillips, 1974

SZARKOWSKI, John. *Looking at Phototographs.* New York: Museum of Modern Art, 1973 (BN) (L/R)

SZARKOWSKI, John. *The Photographer's Eye.* New York: The Museum of Modern Art, 1980 (BN)

SZARKOWSKI, John. *Photography Until Now,* New York: The Museum of Modern Art, 1989 (DG)

TAFT, Robert. *Photography and the American Scene: A social History 1839-1889.* New York: Dover Publications, 1964 (BN)

TAGG, John. *The Burden of Representation: Essays on Photographies and Histories.* London: Macmillan, 1988 (AK)

TAUSK, Peter. *Die Geschichte der Fotografie im 20. Jahrhundert.* Köln: DuMont Buchverlag, 1977; *Historia de la Fotografia en el siglo XX /* Epílogo de Josep Maria Casademont. Barcelona: Gustavo Gili, 1978; *Photography in the 20ᵗ. Century.* London: Focal Press, 1980; (L/R)

TILLMANNS, Urs. *Geschichte der Photographie: ein jahrhundert präsgt ein Medium.* Frauenfeld: Huber, 1981 (MF)

TRACHTENBERG, Alan. *Classic Essays on Photography.* New Haven (Connecticut): Leete's Island Books, 1980 (BN)

TURNER, Peter. *History of Photography.* London: Hamlyn, 1987 (JS)

TURNER, Peter. *Photo Texts /* Gerry BADGER. London: Travelling Light, [1989?]

YOUNGER, Daniel P. (Ed.). *Multiple Views. Logan Grant essays on Photography, 1983-1989.* Albuquerque: University of New Mexico Press, 1991 (MF)

Vanités: photographies de mode des XIXe et XXe siècles. Paris: Centre National de la Photographie, 1993 (MF)
VIGNEAU, André. *Une brève histoire de l'art de Nièpce a nos jours.* Paris: Laffont, 1963 (L/R)

WARNER, Mary. *Photography and Its Critics: A Cultural History, 1839-1900.* Cambridge: Cambridge University, 1997 (AK)

WEAVER, Mike. *The Photographic Art: Pictorial Traditions in Britain and America.* Edinburgh: The Scottish Arts Council, 1986 (IJ)

WEAVER, Mike (Ed.). *The Art of Photography, 1839-1989*. New Haven; London: Yale University, 1989 (MF)

WEIERMAIER, Peter. *Photographie als Kunst 1879-1979, Kunst als Photographie 1949-1979*. Vienna: Vortragssammlung Fotografis, 1979-1980-1981

WELLS, Liz (Ed.). *Photography: A Critical Introduction*. London; New York: Routledge, 1997 (AK) (JS)

WESTERBECH, Colin. *Bystander. A history of street photography*. London: Thames and Hudson, 1994

WHITING, John R. *Photography is a language* (1st ed. 1946). New York: Arno Press, 1979

WILLIAMS, Val. *Women Photographers: The Other Observers 1900 to the Present*. London: Virago Press, 1986

WILLSBERGER, Johann. *Fotofaszination: Kameras, Bilder, Fotografen*. München: Orbis Verlag, 1988

WISSNER, Adolf. *Photographieren eisnt uns jetzt*. München: R. Oldebourg, 1970

WITKIN, Lee D. / Barbara LONDON. *The Photograph Collector's Guide*. Boston: New York Graphic Society, 1979 (BN)

ZANNIER, Italo. *Neorealismo e fotografia*. Udine: Art&, 1987 (MF)

ZANNIER, Italo. *L'Occhio della fotografia: protagonisti, tecniche e stili dell' "invenzione maravigliosa"*. Roma: La Nuova Italia Scientifica, 1988

ZANNIER, Italo. *Storia e tecnica della fotografia: con una antologia di testi*. Roma; Bari: Laterza, 1983

Mariona Fernández, is a librarian at the Centre de Documentació d'Art Contemporani Alexandre Cirici de Barcelona.

Editor
Joan Fontcuberta

Published by
Actar

Translation
Graham Thomson

Graphic design
Montse Sagarra

Production
Font i Prat Associats

Printing
Ingoprint, SA

Distribution
ACTAR
Roca i Batlle, 2
E-08023 Barcelona
Tel: +34 93 418 77 59
Fax: +34 93 418 67 07
info@actar-mail.com

Cover photograph
**Photomontge by Sébastien Loubatié from
an original photograph by Joe Rosenthal**

Double-page photograph
Joseph-Nicéphore Niepce, *View from the window
in Gras,* **1827. Heliography, Gersheim collection,
Humanities Research Center, University of Texas,
Austin.**

ISBN 84-95273-50-0
D.L. B-23086-02